MW01016067

UP IN THE MORNING, OUT ON THE JOB

"Lo and behold—growing up and still growing up in and around Nanaimo."
— *George Dorman*

UP IN THE MORNING, OUT ON THE JOB

The George Dorman Story, Volume I

George Dorman

BRECHIN PUBLISHING
NANAIMO, BC

BRECHIN PUBLISHING
5120 Fillinger Crescent
Nanaimo, BC V9V 1H8

Printed and bound in Canada.

Canadian Cataloguing in Publication Data

Dorman, George, 1925–
  Up in the morning, out on the job

  ISBN 0-9698150-0-X
  1. Dorman, George, 1925– 2. Sawmill workers—British
Columbia—Nanaimo—Biography. I. Title.
FC3849.N35Z49 1994.   971.1'2   C94-910283-0
F1089.5.N35A3 1994

I feel sorry for the people who don't drink. When they wake up in the morning, that's as good as they are going to feel all day long.

—Dean Martin

Up in the mornin' out on the job
Work like the devil for my pay,
But that lucky old sun has nothin' to do
But roll around heaven all day.

Fuss with my woman, toil for my kids,
Sweat 'til I'm wrinkled and gray,
While that lucky old sun has nothin' to do
But roll around heaven all day.

Lawd above, can't you know I'm pinin',
Tears all in my eyes;
Send down that cloud with a silver linin',
Lift me to Paradise.

Show me that river, take me across
And wash all my troubles away,
Like that lucky old sun, give me nothin' to do
But roll around heaven all day.

That Lucky Old Sun
lyrics by Haven Gillespie
copyright Robbins Music Co., 1949.

FOREWORD

I AM WRITING THIS FOR MY OLD PAL, SPEED. I am glad that I can contribute something to his memoirs. It must be fifty years since I first started to call him Speed. I didn't name him that. I don't know where it came from, but it's been a long time.

I can remember when we were in the Navy, in Shelburne, Nova Scotia. George was a real "Jackie" character in those days—a real salt. He used to have the sleeves on his tunic turned up and on the inside of his left sleeve he had red satin lining on the cuff for port and on his right sleeve he had green satin lining on the cuff for starboard. He looked pretty sharp in those days. He was younger and slimmer. We had a great time.

Many a time we went down to the wet canteen and drank quart bottles of Moosehead and Staghead beer they made back there. I think that stuff must have been about twenty percent. Boy, it was strong stuff.

One time when we were shooting craps a stoker was giving George a bad time. George got up to plow him one and missed. His fist went right through a lath and plaster wall. When he went to pull his hand out, he couldn't because the lath wanted to come back out the same way. Consequently, the guy took his time and hit George about four times before we could jump up and stop them. We finally got George's arm out and turned them loose. That was the end of the stoker.

George had some good pals in Shelburne. They were all stokers working in the machine shop and if you ever wanted anything made, a knife or something like that, boy, they were just too happy to make it for you. They either made it or George would make it for us.

After the war, when we came home, we kept up with our friendship. I can remember one time we went up to his cabin at Englishman River Falls to shoot his dog, which had distemper. I can't remember who fired the shot, but the bullet glanced off the top of the dog's forehead and it went down like a stoned steer. Of course everybody thought it was dead, so we walked back to the cabin and started drinking beer. About fifteen minutes later the dog walked into the cabin and he was all covered with blood. Everybody grabbed their guns and I bet you that dog must have weighed 400 pounds he was so full of lead.

Another time, I was up in the kitchen talking to George's mom while she was in the pantry making the boys' lunches. It must have taken her two loaves of bread to make those lunches. All of a sudden, KAPOW! I ran down in the basement and there was George and his brother Fred, target shooting with a .303 in the bloody basement.

A couple of years later when we were all married, George, Johnnie Bohoslowich and I wanted to go duck hunting. We didn't have a car so we decided we were going to go down to what is now called the Anchorage. We rented one of those putt putt boats. We went out there and duck hunting wasn't that great, so we just cruised around. We were shooting sea gulls and shags and everything else that flew by. All of a sudden I heard, "Hey, you guys, get out of there." It was Frank Denton. We ran right through his decoys. He was kind of cheesed off about that.

When we came back into town we were coming down Northumberland Channel and I said, "Jesus, there's Frank Greenfield." He was the game warden, driving a '47 Dodge, a blue one. George said, "That's okay, we'll go down to Departure Bay and fool around there for a couple of hours and he'll get tired of waiting."

But damned if we didn't run out of gas. We paddled into

shore and there was old Greenfield waiting for us at the end of the wharf. He checked out all our guns and, of course, we all had pumps in those days. He checked out the plugs we had as to whether they just had three shells or not. He asked Johnnie his name and Johnnie says, "Bohoslowich." Frank says, "Hey slow down, slow down." So Johnnie had to spell it again for him a lot slower. I thought we were going to jail that time for sure, but old Frank let us off. He was a pretty good guy after all, I guess.

George, Johnnie and I used to go up to the Nanaimo River Canyon, to the El Rancho. We used to drink and dance all night there and about four o'clock in the morning, when it was starting to get daylight, we would take the girls home and go fishing. Lots of times we woke up and found ourselves out there putting around. Everyone was so tired from drinking and dancing the night before we all fell asleep. It seemed to me that we never caught many fish in those days.

It was about the same time that we went up to Horne Lake hunting one night. There was George and I, Pud Ward, Gib Stevens, Fred Dawson and probably some others. George had a bunch of incendiary shells for his .303 and was shooting them off in the rocks at Horne Lake Mountain. It's a wonder we never started a forest fire.

One time George, Johnnie and I started at the Newcastle bar at the beginning of a hunting trip to the Upper Campbell Lakes. We hit every beer parlour from the Newcastle to the Quinsam Hotel in Campbellton. By the time we got up to there we were stoned. We didn't want to pitch the tent that night because it was raining cats and dogs, so we rented a cabin. By the time we got to bed it was the wee hours of the morning. George and Johnnie got up and went hunting, but I said, "No way!" I didn't care if a deer walked up to the cabin door, I wasn't going to get up to shoot it, I was so sick.

They went out hunting, tramped around all bloody day and got soaked to the ass. That wasn't enough; they had to go to Campbell River that night. The game warden stopped them and asked, "Where are you guys going?"

"Oh, we're just going in for some groceries," George said. He shone his flashlight in our car and saw a gun laying on the back seat. "You've got a gun there, eh? Have you got shells in that gun?" George said yes.

"Have you got a flashlight, too?" the game warden wanted to know.

"Yeah," George said.

"Great combination, going hunting and getting groceries," he says, but George talked his way out of that. When they came back into camp George told me me that Johnnie was was shaking like a leaf when the game warden was questioning them. From that time on we all called him Shaky.

I remember one time, I was living up at the Salmon River Bridge and George came up and spent the night with us. The next morning, a Sunday, we went into the Kelsey Bay area hunting. We were stopped on a bridge wondering how we could shoot one of the beef cattle a fellow up there had on his farm. We were discussing how we could shoot one and get it in the truck and out of there before anybody caught us, when this clown came over the bridge about ninety miles an hour and smucked us right in the tailgate. The cops wanted to know what the hell we were doing parked on the bridge. I think George talked us out of that episode too. I don't recall us ever having to pay any fines for it, and if I am not mistaken, I think the guy's insurance had to buy George a new tailgate for his pickup.

One night a bunch of us wanted to go pitlamping, so we took an old Dodge panel truck I bought off Island Industries, who I was working for at the time. We got in this truck and headed off down the road in the pouring rain. "There's a pair of eyes! There's a pair of eyes!" George shouted. I stopped the truck and he got out and ran through the salal and ferns. After awhile he came back, "Naw, he's gone; can't find him."

Down the road a ways he shouted again, "There's a pair of eyes! There's a pair of eyes!" so I stopped the truck and out he got again. This happened several times, but we never did get any deer that night. George sure got soaking wet. There were about four of us in the panel that night and everybody was hoping that he wouldn't shoot a deer because we didn't know if the game warden was up there that weekend. George was the only one who got wet. The rest of us sat in the truck and watched him running through the salal and ferns after these eyes.

I wasn't there the time that he and Johnnie and their wives went out duck hunting at the flats. George and Johnnie got in an argument and Johnnie, to press his point, stuck a shotgun in his belly. That stupid old shotgun never even had a safety on it. It's a wonder he never shot George.

On another hunting trip George, Johnnie and I were down at John Dooley's ranch, at Yellow Point, just past Purdell's farm. We were pheasant hunting and while we were walking through a field we came to an electric fence. George said to Johnnie, "You hold the wire while I step through the fence." Johnnie grabbed hold of that wire and, of course, he got a shock. Was he ever upset. But he didn't have much time to give George hell because a bull came along and chased all three of us right out of the field. We were running and taking our red shirts off as we were ran.

When Johnnie and I were helping George build one of his houses, Johnnie had a little grey Austin. One week he put new tires on it, as well as a brake job and a radiator. I had just come back from Seattle and I brought one of those firecrackers that you put on spark plug wires. The three of us were going to go and have a beer after we finished work. Johnnie fired his Austin up and Sshhhh, POW! A big cloud of blue smoke came out from under the hood. He jumped out of the car and said, "What do you think it is, George?"

"I don't know John, it sounds like you blew a piston." Of course when Johnnie lifted up the hood and saw the wires and the piece of firecracker that was left. He said, "Oh, somebody played a trick on me. Somebody played a trick on me." He was so happy that his car hadn't blown up that he didn't care about somebody pulling a trick on him.

One time Johnnie and I went out fishing with George in his boat after work. I don't know if Johnnie never worked that day or if he got off early, but when we picked him up at the Newcastle he was three sheets to the wind. We went out fishing and, by God, if he didn't fall overboard. I reached over and opened the throttle and took off in the boat. But George said, "Gee, you can't do that!" He let off on the throttle and we went around and picked up Johnnie. I was all for leaving that clown out there to swim for shore. He was just a bloody nuisance when he was drinking in those days.

One night George and I had been out drinking beer and were parked in front of his house talking. It was a nice night, and we were sitting with the windows down. George was telling me about all the girls he had been screwing before he was married, when his first wife June stuck her head in the window and said, "Oh, is that right, George?" I just about shit myself right there. I never did hear what she said to him after she got him in the house. I'm hoping to find out from his memoirs.

ANDY POJE
Nanaimo, B.C.
1993

1

I CAME INTO THIS WORLD as a result of some unusual circumstances. My father George was wounded at Vimy Ridge, late in the First World War. He was left for dead on the battlefield, but twenty-six hours later a stretcher bearer noticed he was alive and picked him up. He was paralyzed from the waist down, and spent two and a half years recovering in the Tooting military hospital in England. My mother, Bridgette Marie Gertrude O'Reilly, who was from Dublin, nursed him during this period. They were married in 1919 and shortly afterwards moved to Canada.

My parents' first baby, a boy, died at an early age because, my mother was convinced, he had been born in a hospital. From then on she had her children at home, which was at 4774 Booth Street in South Vancouver. First, my two sisters Dorothy and Marge came along, followed by myself and two brothers, Fred and Reg.

While all this was going on my father had been getting back on his feet again. He had grown up on Bowen Island, where there were and still are lots of Dormans, and worked as a logger before the war. When he came home with my mother, they went back to Bowen for a short time, but he soon realized that because of his injuries, he needed to get into a different kind of work. He went to Vancouver and trained in the Red Cross workshops, to be a metalwork and woodwork teacher. His first job was in Nanaimo in 1925 and he taught at Harewood school and other schools around Nanaimo. He was instrumental in building the Harewood Manual Training Building, which was all built by volunteer labour, and then he set up a night school to teach older people woodworking and the other skills they needed to build their own homes.

My father was also the first school maintenance worker for the City of Nanaimo. He had a crew of men that used to do the maintenance work; some of those men are still working at it today.

Of course, as we grew up, my brothers and I had to follow along and do a lot of this woodworking too, so we became very good at it. When I was about eight years old, in 1933, my dad put my brothers and I to work digging out the basement of a house we rented on the corner of Howard and Fifth Street.

The house was up on posts and we were digging it out to put in foundations and make a basement. To make it easier we had taken some of the braces off the posts. One day, right around Christmas time, a bad storm came up with a wind that was blowing 100 miles an hour.

Fred and I came out of school and went home. My mother was home and, I am sure my sisters and Reg were at school. Fred and I went into the basement, as we always did when we came out of school around three o'clock, and put some wood into the wood furnace. When we came out to lock the door, it didn't want to fit into the frame. We went up the back stairs and just as we were opening the door to go into the kitchen the house slid over sideways off its foundation. It skidded over sideways about eight feet, the height of all the posts in the basement from which we had taken the braces.

Fred ran down through the kitchen and hallway. I ran into the pantry, where all of the dishes rained down on me. I've still got a scar on my right wrist and another one on my back near my spine where I was cut by broken dishes. Then the house started filling up with smoke. I took a punch at the window in the front and blood was flying off my hand from the cut I got from the dishes. Fred was a little smarter than I and got the baseball bat after he saw all the blood flying off my hand, and smashed out a window in the door.

My dad came limping across with all the grade twelve students from the manual training class. He had a mattock in his hand and chopped that door apart in about two seconds flat. The grade twelve class was a big bunch of healthy boys who got us out of there and managed to somehow get the furnace put out. It was quite an exciting time. The house is still there today.

When my father first got his job in Nanaimo, he lived here for three years before the rest of the family moved over. He stayed with a family by the name of Lowe, and they lived right around the corner on Harewood Road, the second house down. They had a lot of land there, five acres, and their place was called Five Acres.

So there was the Dorman family, with its house fallen over in a howling blizzard just before Christmas. Bill Lowe invited us to move in with them. It snowed all night and all next day and the snow was thirty-three inches deep on the flat, with drifts up to eight feet deep. There was no school for quite some time.

Finally, about three weeks later, they got the house jacked back up again and got a foundation under it. That was one of our most exciting Christmases, I guess. The Lowe family looked after us very well.

Through the '30s we had a good friend by the name of Dan Buchanan, who had a cabin at Great Central Lake. My dad helped him build a boat. We went up there quite a few times a year, mostly in the summer. We would go up there for a weekend. One time, when I was eight, I was going there alone with my dad, who was driving. I believe we had an old '33 Essex at the time. Along Cameron Lake the road was all pot holes and rougher than hell. It wasn't a very good night; it was raining. My dad went around a corner a little too fast and he pot-holed right off the road. I was sitting in the back with all the groceries. I ended up with my backside in the groceries, which broke a few tomatoes and other things. Apart from that, the car wasn't too bad. Somebody came along and pulled us out, and we managed to motor on with a bent fender or two.

When we got to the lake Dan had just painted the boat that

my dad had built. They were going to teach me how to row. They tied a long rope between the boat and the dock. They'd push the boat out from the dock, then I'd have to row back. After doing this about ten times I had learned how to row a boat. I think it took most of the weekend. I wasn't very old at the time, eight or nine.

When we were living in Nanaimo the fellow who used to run Nanaimo Creamery, Cyril Randle, had one of those little clinker built boats that Lake & Son made. He used to take us out fishing in it. We all liked that so much we built ourselves a little row boat. We used to go out from Departure Bay as far as the buoys and come back in along the inside channel by the biological station. One night when we were coming in through there I caught a ten or twelve pound salmon. That was the first salmon I ever caught.

In school I flunked grade one, so brother Fred caught up with me and we were in the same class after that. During my school years my dad had an idea he was going to make a manual training teacher out of me. Part of this involved my having to wear short pants, right up to grade ten. The only other kid who had to wear short pants was Bobby Burns. When I started going around with my hands in my pockets, my dad had my mother sew the pockets up. I wasn't too happy about this and was kidded about it constantly. This still sticks in my mind. My dad sure as hell heard lots about it before he died, but thinking back on it, I guess it didn't hurt me.

Another kid in our class was Cecil Dunn. His father used to make a lot of wine, as did a lot of people around there, particularly the Italians. The Dunn boys were always taking the odd bottle. One day, probably when we were in grade seven or eight, Cecil got some wine which he and Fred drank. They were all giggled up in school and no one could figure out what was wrong with them. I don't think the teachers knew, but there was no more of that happening.

Davy Peffers, Cecil Dunn and I, and some of the Italian boys thought we knew how to make wine so we picked all these blackberries 'til hell wouldn't have it. Lots of them grew wild all over the area around our home. They were the big, thorny ones. We mushed them all up and added sugar. We scrounged up all these wine bottles with corks and lids and put the mixture in them. We didn't know it had to ferment first in a bigger container.

Previous to this my father had me build a little cabin in our back yard to practice my carpentry skills. There was a little loft in it and underneath that we hid all these wine bottles. After a few days they started exploding, and every time I went to check on them another one would have blown up. Our first go at making wine wasn't very successful, and when we did try some it tasted like vinegar. That was the end of wine making for me until later in my life.

We used to play a lot of soccer in school, and one of our teachers used to give us an hour off classes every now and then to go out and play soccer. One morning Fred stepped on the ball, fell over and broke his ankle. I was pretty strong by this time, so I picked him up and packed him all the way home. My mother and dad had to get the doctor, who put a cast on Fred's ankle. Poor old Fred, he suffered a long time over that bad ankle.

During the Hungry Thirties, when I lived in Harewood, people on welfare had to work to get their relief money, building roads, bridges and other public benefits. In the Englishman River Falls area there was a big relief camp with about thirty men working there. They carried on with the relief camps for quite some time. As a matter of fact, they were still there when I went off and started working myself.

I got a letter from Tommy Douglas one time asking what I thought about people working instead of collecting Unemployment Insurance and sitting home watching TV. That was one of the things the CCFers in the '30s, and later the NDPers thought. They think people should stay home and get paid for doing nothing. In the '30s, Harewood was all gravel roads and the relief workers worked on the roads and ditches with picks and shovels for their money.

I wrote back to Douglas: "I've been in business for thirty years now and I find most often when I get one of these guys who have been on Unemployment Insurance for six or eight months, they can't work they're so out of shape. Even if you give them twenty-eight days they still can't shape up. As far as I'm concerned, Tommy, I think you're going to pay Unemployment Insurance whether they work the whole time or not, but they should work enough to keep in shape." He never did write me back.

A lot of my dad's wartime friends had got farms at Errington, not far from this relief camp, and in the early '30s we started going up there a lot. One of our closest friends was a family named Taylor, and we used to stay on their farm. They had a great old hand-hewn log house, which today is at Craig's Heritage Centre in Parksville. It was made out of huge logs. I used to sleep in that house, for about six years, right inside the front door on the left. Us three boys used to sleep in the same bed together there, Fred, Reg and I. Lots of memories in that old house.

The farmer, Jim Taylor, had a contract to provide all the vegetables for the relief camp. They had about ten acres of root vegetables. They also had all kinds of pigs, so we used to slaughter these pigs, then scald them in boiling water, skin them, and cut them in half.

They didn't have a pickup truck, just a car with the back seat out of it. We'd pile these pork halves in the back of the car, and Fred and I often got to go with Jim to the camp. I don't know if Reg ever did, but we used to take turns. We used to go into Englishman River Falls with vegetables and eggs, butter, milk and cream which was also supplied by the Taylor farm. Every night we had to take something in to the camp. It was so interesting because in my lifetime most people haven't seen something like a relief camp, and will never see it.

The Taylors had a permit from the game department to shoot the deer because they were eating all the relief workers' food. They were allowed to shoot them at night—pitlamping it was called.

There used to be so many deer in that Englishman River Falls area. In the winter time all the bucks would come down from the mountains and you could go in there any time in November to January, and see any amount of huge deer with great horns. It would flabbergast most guys if they ever knew how it used to be.

I was hunting on the Taylor farm with my father one night,

before I did any shooting, and we went down to the garden. Next to it was a great big oat field. We were walking along and we spotted this deer out in the oats. We got up close to it and could see it was a big buck. My father had a little forked stick which he propped his gun up on and I stood behind him and held the light. My dad goes, "POW!" Down goes the deer. We started walking over there; my dad couldn't move all that well because he had a game leg. When we got over there, I shone the light into the oats and I saw these eyes. I said to my dad, " Hey, you missed it." So my dad up and fires again. No more eyes. We walked ahead about ten feet into the oats and there's a five pointer deader than hell.

We thought that was great. We gutted the deer and my dad stayed there. I went back up and got Mr. Taylor and we came back and got that deer. We took it up to the barn, hung it up, gutted it and so forth.

The following weekend we went up to stay again. Mr. Taylor said to my dad, "Hey, George, you won't believe what I found."

"Well," my dad said. "What did you find?"

"I was cutting that oat field the other day and I ran into a deer not twenty feet away from where you shot that other five pointer."

"Your kidding," my dad said. "What was it?"

"Another five pointer." Here there were two five pointers and we thought there was only one. Of course, the meat was all ruined, but we looked at the horns. It had better horns than the one we found.

We shot a lot of deer up around Errington during the Depression. The Dorman family just about lived off it at times and what we didn't eat we gave away or bartered for something else we needed. All the ladies used to get together when we had a lot of deer and bottle the deer meat. They cut it up, cooked it and put it into jars. Then they boiled the jars for a while, took them out and let them cool. That's how they used to keep deer meat in the '30s and into the '40s because there were no freezers at that time. It tasted very good; I've eaten a lot of bottled deer meat in my time.

Once when we were leaving the farm to go back to Harewood a two-point deer ran across the road and into the front of the car. We got out and I pounded on its head with a rock until we thought it was dead. My dad said, "We'll gut it when we get home." We put the deer in the trunk of the car, and drove home. When we got home the deer was making noises in the trunk. We got into the back yard an my dad opened up the trunk. Out jumped the two-pointer, and started running all around in the back yard. We had a big high fence there and it couldn't get over the fence. After chasing it around for a while my dad finally got out the .22 and shot it.

One of the funniest things to happen at the Taylor farm was a trick we played on our dad. Fred and I thought up this one. Our dad was in the house one night having a beer with Mr. Taylor. Fred and I got an old two-gallon maple syrup can. We cut a couple of little holes in it, about the size and distance apart of deer eyes. We put a little candle inside the can.

There was a big orchard on the Taylor farm, with a bit of a field behind it that was full of deer at night. They used to come in to the orchard, too. This night, Fred and I went out, lit the candle, put the can up on the stump, and called our dad. "Hey, dad, you should see the deer." My dad came out with his .30-.30. He rested it on the fence; I was holding the light for him. POW! Nothing happened, so he went POW a second time. The gun was only a single shot so it took a bit to reload it.

In the meantime, Fred started laughing and my dad got mad and said, "What are you laughing about?"

"We were just going to see how good you shoot, Chief," I said. "There's a can over there with two holes and a candle in it." Well, that was a howl for years after. My dad just couldn't get over Fred and I dreaming up this scheme. He wasn't upset; he had to laugh about it. Both bullets he fired hit the can, but didn't shoot the candle out.

My dad had a friend who was a fur trader and worked for a company called R.J. Pop, in Vancouver. Every year they had a hunters and trappers party in Vancouver and he used to ask my dad, "Do you think you can get us a deer or two?" I was not allowed to have a gun at that time and we were hunting with Mr. Taylor, who had an old double-barrel shotgun.

We went up to Digby swamp and were walking along

early in the morning with daylight coming. It was quite foggy. All of a sudden a four-point buck came out of the brush and stood looking at us from about forty feet away. My friend only had bird shot, but I had some shotgun shells in my pocket.

"Hey, try these two," I said. He up and fired one shot and the deer went down. "What kind of shells are those?" he asked.

I told him about our friend Bill Lowe, who worked for the Canadian Collieries in their shop in Nanaimo. He always got us ball bearings to play with from the shop. Fred and I took apart some of the shotgun shells, took out the lead shot and put some ball bearings in. There was room for two ball bearings.

My dad sent the deer over to Vancouver and sometime later he got a letter back from the fur trader at R.J. Pop, with two ball bearings in it. "Hey, George," it said. "What do you shoot your deer with over there on the Island? I have never seen shot like this before." That was a great joke in the Errington area.

A lot of raccoons used to come into the Taylor's orchard and one of us kids' jobs was to shoot them. One winter when we were staying there, the Taylor's German shepherd treed five raccoons three different times. They were all dead in the end. The main reason they wanted all the raccoons killed was because they used to cause so much trouble with the chickens. He wanted to get rid of these raccoons, so us kids had a field day doing that.

One day I was hunting with my .22, before I graduated to rifles and shotguns. I was hunting with Jim Taylor and he and I were in the bush. I looked up and there was a raccoon up a big fir tree, on a limb about forty feet up.

Every time I aimed my gun at it and was about to pull the trigger, the raccoon would put its paws up over its eyes. Mr. Taylor said to me, "I can't believe that. Put it down and do it again." I put the gun down and the raccoon looked at me again with a dumb look on its face. I put the gun up again and it would do the same thing.

"Hey," I said to him. "I'm not going to shoot that raccoon."

"Don't bother shooting it George," he said. "It's about two miles from my chickens, so I don't think it will make it there this winter."

One day when I was about twelve years old I was walking

with my father and brother Fred on the Taylor farm. It was pouring rain on a Saturday afternoon and the farmer's dog scared up a bird which we could not see. My father reminded me how to use the .22 and sent me after it. This was the first time I was allowed to shoot when he wasn't standing beside me. I took the gun and ran into the bush where the barking was going on. When I got to the dog, I looked in the tree and about sixteen feet up was this cock pheasant staring at us. I shot it in the head and down it came. I brought it out to my dad and he had a fit. He said they had just started releasing pheasants to get them started on Vancouver Island. The damage was already done, so we took the bird home and ate it.

In 1937, we managed to buy our own property at Errington. It was 160 acres, mostly covered with bush and timber, about a mile and a half from Englishman River Park. We three boys were always allowed to bring a pal or two with us when we went up there on weekends. It was a great environment for young boys to grow up.

We had our own little stream just a short ways from the log cabin we built. There were always plenty of deer around, and fish in our own stream. My father would tell my two brothers, "You go and catch some fish. And you, George, take the .22 and see if you can shoot a couple of grouse for dinner." It was a matter of getting three bullets, and you'd better come back with two birds.

We went up there for years and did a lot of hard work clearing land and putting in a garden. My father always had us kids helping or doing something on his friends' farms. Everything was more or less a barter business in those days. We used to get potatoes and any amount of carrots and other root vegetables from the farm and we had a nice little stash of them at home in Harewood. Most often things were traded for something else; for work or woodwork or something. That was the way of life in the '30s.

At our farm we had some neighbours named Morrison. There were two ladies living on this farm and we were allowed to go down there and duck hunt. These people were very nice friends and there was nobody working the farm at that time. It was always interesting to go down and see two little ladies, and it was great just knowing nice people like them. There were a lot of older people living in the Errington area at the time. When I go up there today and see all the hippie shacks, and see what a mess it is, it makes me barf.

We used to get all kinds of ducks on the Morrison farm. My dad's rule was, "You have three shells; you make sure you bring home two ducks." Quite often I used to fall behind. When that happened I'd go down there first thing in the morning, just at daylight. I'd find a whole bunch of ducks close together in the water, then sneak up on them as best I could. I had an old $4.00 hammer gun that my father bought me at an auction sale. I'd cock the two hammers, sneak up as close as I could get, and give them a whap. Sometimes I got eight or ten at a time. Then I had enough ducks to waste a few shells practising wing shooting. I wasn't all that good at wing shooting to start with, but I got better as time went on.

One morning after it had snowed about six inches Fred and I went out at daylight to get some ducks on the Morrison property. There were always ducks there. Fred had picked up an old double-barrelled shotgun sometime before that and he had it with him.

I said to Fred, "We gotta get through the fence and charge those ducks 'cause they're too far away."

"OK," he said. "We'll charge them." We crawled through the fence and I guess Fred poked his gun in the snow. He was on my left. We charged and made about forty feet before the ducks flew. They made another twenty feet before we shot, so we didn't gain much. When Fred fired, one gun barrel peeled back like a musket. That gun always had a bad habit of both barrels going off at once and they did this time. I was lucky some of the shrapnel didn't hit me because I was on the right and it was the right barrel that peeled back. We got five of those ducks, three mallards and two widgeons, so we got something out of it. After a while we sawed the barrels off, which was illegal, of course, so we dumped that gun after a few years.

At about the same time I was walking up a road on the mountain behind Errington with my $4.00 shotgun hunting grouse, by myself. A couple of small cedars had blown down across the road and I crawled through them. As I got through a great, bloody black bear roared up on its hind legs. Well, that scared the stuffing right out of me. It was so close to me I could smell its stinky breath.

I cocked both hammers. There was buckshot in one barrel and bird shot in the other. I gave him the buckshot right in the throat first, and then the bird shot when he was falling down. That bear took off and ran over the hill and into some scrub bush. Later that day we came up with Mr. Taylor, who brought his big German shepherd. We found the bear, dead. That was my first encounter with bears.

Shortly after this adventure, my dad, Fred and I went deer hunting and looking for grouse up the same road. When we came to a fork in the road I went up to the left and my dad and Fred walked straight along. I was going up a steep hill, in two or three inches of snow, to a burned-off area farther up. I looked over a bank to the left and there was a five-point buck walking along a blown down, burnt cedar snag. The buck didn't see me and it kept on walking down the log that was off the ground about two feet.

"I'm going to get this guy," I thought. I had my dad's single shot .30-.30. Just as I went to fire, the deer looked at me. It leaped off the log and booted down the road toward where my dad and Fred were. I fired at it, and lucked out. I shot it straight through the heart and it went end over end. I've always considered this my first real deer. I had shot five before this, at night with Mr. Taylor. But this was the first in daylight, and by myself.

I didn't hear any hollering from my dad or Fred after firing the one shot. I had been taught long before how to gut deer, so I gutted it. I knew the road went down quite a ways, so I thought I'd carry on a bit further. There was a bit of timber up there, so I went into the timber to circle around. I was walking out of the scrub timber, where they hadn't logged, with salal up to my belly button or higher, and I heard the sound of something coming towards me. I stopped on a bit of a deer trail and a spike buck came running right at me, going flat out along the deer trail. I guess Fred and my dad had scared it. It wasn't ten feet away when I shot it right in the head. It blew most of its head away. Now I had two bucks.

I grabbed the second one and dragged it out to the top of the road so that Fred could give me a hand when he got there, and gutted it. I finished just as my dad and Fred came along.

"What else did you get?" my dad asked.

"What do you mean, I only fired two shots?" My dad was always going on about wasting bullets because they cost so much money. "I think I got another one, you guys better come along and give me a hand." They couldn't believe it and were shouting and pounding me on the back. My dad was a pretty excitable guy anyway, so this really got him going. That deer was so heavy—170 or 180 pounds—that my dad and I used our belts to tie it to a pole and pack it down the mountain.

The year the San Francisco Bay bridge opened, 1936, my dad and mom stuffed us five children in the car and went down to the opening. We had an Essex at the time. We made that trip again in 1937, and that time went all the way down to Tijuana, Mexico.

All us kids would tell my dad to step on it and pass all the oil tankers. My mom just about had a canary. We used to get my dad going and he would pass them just to get a giggle out of us kids. It was so hot, when we got to Tijuana, that we had to try something we'd heard about.

We had a little trunk on the back of the car where we kept some food. My dad got out some eggs and cooked them on the sidewalk. It was hot enough to cook them, all right. I thought that was real funny.

In 1937, we had a change of cars and got a Zephyr. One day not long after we got it I was riding Butch Branchie home on the crossbar of my bicycle. Around Park and Albert streets, Reg went by in the new Zephyr. He was going to get gas in it and had another boy with him. I don't know what happened, but he lost control of the car. There was a little bit of a dip in the hill there in Harewood Road going up by the Lutheran church, and Reg managed to slide into a pole and bend a front fender.

Sunday nights in the summer time we would go down to Departure Bay and have a picnic. I remember this one time we were playing there and my sister, Dorothy and I were having a teeter totter on an old piece of plank my dad found on the beach.

Dorothy jumped off and the plank came down and hit me across the "bugle." That was my first broken nose.

That same night my mom said she wanted to learn to drive, so my dad let her get behind the wheel. Us noisy kids were in the car and we were down by the Kin Hut. There used to be a house down there with a nice little white fence.

My dad said to my mom, "Okay, back up now. This is what you do." So my mom backed up and my dad said, "Okay. Put the brake on."

Instead of putting the brake on, she put her foot on the gas and pickets were flying in all directions—making another little chore for George to come and fix up a few days later. We had to go down and mend the fence for the fellow, and that was the end of my mom's driving. I don't think she did any more driving after that.

The next driving incident in the Dorman family was when my sister Marge was driving along Howard Avenue and somebody came along Third Street and broad-sided her. That slowed her driving down for a while. That was the old Zephyr again. It was getting banged up quite a bit, but that Zephyr, it lasted for quite some time.

Reg had always been allowed to drive even though he was three years younger than me and I was never allowed to. But one day my dad says, "You go ahead, George, you back the car up." We were using the Zephyr for pulling cedar poles up to build our log cabin. I was backing up and had the door open so I could see where I was going. I didn't notice a root sticking up and pretty soon—no door! No more driving for George, either. Reg got back on the controls and that was the end of my driving on the farm.

In the winter of 1939–40 Fred and I stayed over one night with Jim Taylor because we were going hunting together early the next morning. The Taylors had a hired hand from Denmark by the name of Lars. He was great with us boys and was always helping us to do things. He lived in a little tiny shack, about ten by twelve, with a bunk in it. He worked on the farm in the garden, and with the cows, pigs and chickens.

This morning, Fred and I went over with Mr. Taylor to the huge barn they had. I was walking behind and Mr. Taylor was carrying the lamp. He had to feed some animals before we could go hunting; then he had to come back and milk the cows and some other things, so we didn't have that much time for hunting. We were walking down a narrow passageway that ran through the middle of the barn, with stacks of hay on both sides.

I looked up and saw Lars hanging off a rope. He had climbed up on the hay pile and hooked the rope over a beam, then jumped down and hung himself. This fellow had worked on that farm for about three years. He had saved enough money to bring his mom and dad out from Denmark, but the Germans had gone into Denmark and taken over the country. He got word from his sister that his mom and dad were killed and he couldn't handle it. That's why he hung himself. That was the first dead man I saw. Mr. Taylor climbed up and cut him down. Fred and I had to help lower him down onto the ground, then we went and got the police.

One of our pals we were allowed to take up to the Errington farm was Frank Branchi. One day he and I were hunting in the rain down next to the Digby swamp property when we heard the Taylor's dog barking. We ran toward the sound. I stopped running for a minute to cock my old $4.00 shotgun. I could see the bird and the dog in the distance. Butch ran in front of me and my gun went off. It just missed his ear by about six inches. That was a great scare for me, the only one with guns that I ever had.

Another time, when my father had sent me off with my .22 to get some grouse right close to our cabin, I was down in the swamp and the dog ran off barking at a grouse. The grouse flew away and the next minute the dog came running back with what I first thought were two cows chasing him. The dog ran right back to me and I saw that it was a cow elk and a calf. We had quite a laugh about that when I went up and told my dad. I don't think he really believed me.

A little while later that same year he and I went down to the Morrison's to hunt some ducks one night. We were hiding in the bushes and the next moment, lo and behold, there was a big seven-point bull elk that came out of the same spot where I had seen the cow and the calf. It wandered out right close to my dad and I. Suddenly it smelled us and went wandering back into the bush. Those were my first experiences of sighting elk.

At the Branch #10 Legion in Nanaimo there was a twenty-yard rifle range in the basement. My father used to take me there constantly to sharpen up my shooting. We used single-shot, heavy-barreled Cooey .22s for target shooting. We had a great time learning how to take our time and shoot straight. If you got all ten shots in the bull's eye it was called a possible. I was so steady at that time that I continuously shot possibles. I learned how to shoot well there and I still take my time; I am not in a great hurry when I shoot. I get a good aim instead of missing.

When I was thirteen years old my dad and I went out on the opening of deer season. We went up our favourite logging road by our cabin. The sun was just coming up and shining down into this little clearing and there was the biggest five-point buck you would ever want to see. It was just standing there. I shot at it with deadly aim and it bolted. We never bothered to go after it.

I wasn't too smart at that time, but after my many years of hunting I've seen lots of deer bolt just like that one. I finally learned to track them down. I can think of any amount of them that I went after, and it turned out I had hit them. They would have been shot in the heart. They ran maybe 100 yards and there they were, dead. When I reflect back on that big deer, I know I hit it and it ran away and died, but at that time I hadn't had that experience. I don't think my father had either or he would have known to chase after it.

There used to be a lot of cascara trees around Errington and we cut a lot of bark. It was made into Exlax medicine and we gathered it to sell and make a few dollars. We would put it in sacks, thirty or forty pounds each, and sell it in Nanaimo.

One time my friend Dave Peffers and I found some cascara around Nanaimo. We cut a bunch and put it in a bag, along with a thirty-three pound rock. We sold it to a Mr. Savage, who ran Buckerfields in Nanaimo at the time. About three weeks later he phoned me up and said, "Hey, George I think you owe me some money. I found a rock in your cascara bark." We had taken a lot of bark into this man and he got to thinking, "How come this bag weighs so much more than the others?" The bag was more or less the same size as the others. He prodded it with a rod and found this big round rock in the middle of it. My father made me walk all the way down there. I never even had a bike in those days and had to walk all the way down to Buckerfield's which is still there today, down by the Occidental Hotel. I had to go back and give him his money. We were only getting six cents a pound and I had to give him around $2.00 back for the rock. After that we got a little smarter, and put sand in with the bark to make it weigh a pound or two more. All in all, we cut hundreds of pounds of cascara bark up through the Errington area.

At Errington, besides cutting cascara bark and helping the farmers in exchange for vegetables, we also made a lot of shakes. Cedar shakes, barn shakes as we used to call them. They were thirty inches long, all hand split. We also made a lot of fence posts, all hand split. One time my dad got a job for the Old Log Cabin Inn that used to be right on the beach in Qualicum. They needed a new shake roof so we made all the shakes for that roof. Those shakes were all forty-two inches long and we had to find some good cedar to make them. On our property, right beside our log cabin, we had a nice big cedar tree. It was twelve and a half feet in diameter and it was all burned out on the inside.

My dad kept an eye on Fred and I and told us what to do. I got inside the tree with our little five-foot saw. It started out as a seven-foot bucking saw, but my dad cut two feet off, it so it was only a five-foot saw. Fred was holding on to the other end of the saw on the outside and we cut down that huge cedar snag. The butt end was kind of tough so we made it into fence posts and split the rest of it into shakes.

That used to be one of our chores. I made so many shakes I can't even start counting them. We did the same thing when we had time at home around Nanaimo. We cut any amount of dead snags from around all the dams, around the army camp, and anywhere we could find them. What with making fence posts, cutting shakes and cutting firewood we had a busy time, Fred and I. Reg was younger then, and he didn't get in on much of the wood cutting.

Once I split some wood on our farm to make cedar decoys. I made mallard decoys after studying the mallards in our back yard. I cut them out just the way the mallards looked and painted them all up. They looked great. About the second time I used them I was hunting with Fred and Wally Newberry. I put the decoys out in the water and we were sitting around waiting for ducks to come in. A bunch landed away off to the left so Fred and Wally went down after them.

While I was waiting, some ducks came in and I shot a couple. The others kept going beyond my decoys and landed. I was sneaking up on them when I heard three shots. I walked back to see what had happened and here were Fred and Wally with the reddest faces you ever saw. The silly bastards had sneaked up on my twelve decoys, which cost me about six months to build, and blew the hell out of them. I had to do a little putty job on them and repaint them to make them as good as new. I was glad they didn't sink from all the lead that was in them.

In Nanaimo during the '30s there was a farmers' market that was open in the summer, under the Bastion Street bridge. We opened up a stall one summer to sell things I made in our workshop at home—wheelbarrows, ironing boards, medicine cabinets, cedar chests, boxes, towel racks, bird houses, tables, my dad's famous crib boards, boot pullers, boxes, and Christmas tree stands (which I still make for friends today). Making and selling these knick-knacks at the market was my first real business experience. I made them and put them together, leaving it to whoever bought them to paint them. You have some of that happening today in Nanaimo, but there is not so much of it any more like there used to be.

My dad had a good friend down in Chemainus who was in local sales at the sawmill. He used to get all these short pieces of boards and save them for my dad. Very seldom was a piece any longer than five feet. They were clear cedar with some fir and pine amongst them. We used them to make knick-knacks. My dad used to pay a small amount of money to this fellow for these short pieces, which is where most of our wood supply came from.

On one occasion my dad and I were going down to get a

load of boards and we had the back seat out of the '37 Zephyr. Just before we got to the Chemainus mill the front right tire blew and we went skidding into a maple tree—it is still standing today. Another ding for the old Zephyr. We changed the tire and somebody came along and pulled us out of the ditch. Every time we used that Zephyr it seemed we put another ding in it. My mom used to get quite vexed with us over the bills for dings in the Zephyr. It cost a lot of money to keep that Zephyr running, I can assure you.

Another thing we built a lot were skis. My dad used to get one-by-four spruce from a friend. We used the table saw to cut a groove down the middle, and cut them off at seven feet or whatever we wanted. We put water into a bucket over a fire in our back yard and would stick the end of the one-by-four in the boiling water. We boiled the stuffing out of it, then we'd put it into this jig my dad had made. The odd one broke, but not very many. Then we used to put a piece of leather over the ski. It was like putting on a moccasin, you just put your foot under the strap. This is what we used to ski with; no ski boots, no nothing. Whatever we had, we wore.

We used to ski up above where Malaspina College is today. That was the best ski hill. We used to walk all the way up there, then ski down the hill. One time I didn't even make it as far as where Malaspina College is today and my ski came off. It kept on going all the way to Wakesiah Avenue. I had to walk all the way down in the snow and get that ski back. I got to thinking that time that skiing was not really for me, but I kept on with it for a while. After I went into the Navy I didn't think about skiing again until about into the '70s.

One of the things my father did during the '30s, with the help of other people, was to build seven houses for his friends in Nanaimo. Two of the houses were for a fellow by the name of Schwartz, a camera man, and Ronny Squires. They bought some old buildings from the military base out at Nanoose Bay. They used to make munitions out there and they bought two of these big administration buildings, tore them down and kept the lumber. That's what we used to build their two houses on Vancouver Avenue, a block apart.

One of the nicest persons we built a house for was Albert Sutton, who lived two doors down the road from us. He had an old Wee McGregor gas saw for cutting firewood. This saw had a little putt-putt motor on it. You just started it up and it sawed away by itself with a big long heavy blade. We cut a lot of wood all over the place with this saw.

Albert had a little trailer, and one time Hydro cut a right-of-way up this side of Nanoose. There was a bunch of good sized fir on that right-of-way and they gave us the trees for firewood just for taking them away. We cut wood up there and brought it home in the trailer. We had a big wood furnace in Harewood and so did he. We always had stacks of firewood for our own use.

One day, coming home from Nanoose, with Albert towing this trailer with his Model A along Bowen Road, a tire blew on the turn and into the bushes we went. We weren't hurt too much, but we dumped all the wood over. We got the trailer repaired and went back and picked up the wood.

Some other people by the name of Fraser, who lived behind Harewood School in a house we built, would buy four or five cords of alder off my brother and I every year. We went up where all the city dams and reservoirs are, which is kind of a park now, and cut the alder every year. We used to have trouble getting it down, so Albert said, " You guys can use my trailer." He was working on weekends, so we got his trailer and we had a whole bunch of pals who would pull the trailer up there by hand and pull it back down behind Harewood School, which was a matter of three-quarters of a mile or so. That's how we got the four or five cords of wood down to him every year. We had all kinds of guys wanting to pull the trailer and help with it—Davy Peffers, Frank Branchi and Butch Branchini.

Albert built a cabin out at First Lake, back from the lake just a bit, right close to where the Nanaimo River flows out. We kids, when we were younger, got to go up there. We used to swim in the river and catch all kinds of fish. Albert used to tell us all kinds of tales. He worked for Crown Zellerbach and was the fellow who surveyed and did a lot of engineering work on all the timber all up through to Fourth Lake. He used to tell us all kinds of stories about all the deer, the cougar and the elk he saw up there. He was a great friend and so was his wife.

After Crown Zellerbach got going, some of the guys couldn't fit into the logging, and Albert and a bunch of the older fellows used to work in a little sawmill making ties for the railroad. They used to haul all the logs out of Nanaimo Lakes by railroad into Ladysmith in those years, and Albert was working in this little mill cutting ties for it. One day he was behind the saw and somehow the sawyer didn't see him. He dragged Albert back through the saws and sawed him in three pieces. He was sixty-four. That didn't sit very well with the Dorman family or a lot of other people at Crown Zellerbach. Having all these old men who had no experience working on a sawmill wasn't a very good idea.

When we were lads going to school in Five Acres, we did a lot of fishing in the Chase River. At the head of the Chase River there were big falls, from the dams. The first one we called the Number One Dam. I went fishing below the falls quite often by myself and caught a lot of fish. We called the dam above Number One, Number Two. The dam at the top end of Harewood Road, where the spillway is which is now part of the city water system, we called dam Number Three. There was a fellow living there who looked after the dams. His name was Cunningham and he was a big fat fellow. We were convinced there were more fish in the reservoirs, although we were not allowed to fish behind the dams. Cunningham was always hollering at us to get out of there. Another good spot where we were allowed to fish was right where his house was at the Number Three Dam. There was a spillway there that went across the road. It used to be a real good spot. The best time was when the fish spawned in the spring. That is when you used to get a lot of nice big fish. All those rivers and little streams that come out of the lakes are where the fish spawn, and they are always a good place to fish.

We got ourselves a lot of fish at the dams there as well as a lot of lip off old Cunningham. We didn't have any decent poles in those days, just willow sticks with a bit of line, split shots and a hook. If Cunningham chased us and we had to run, we would throw them away. We could easily make another one.

One day Davy Peffers and I went fishing in Chase River, just down the road from our place. We started fishing up from the bridge at Howard Avenue and when we got up close to the falls I ran ahead of Davy to the next pool. It was pretty dried up at the time and the water was real low. I looked in and saw this great big fish, so I put my line in. I guess I was a little impatient, because when the fish took a bite at the hook, I gave a whip on it. The hook came out of its mouth, flew up and caught in a limb. Davy was coming around the corner and he was going to get his line in there. I didn't have time to untangle my line, but the hook still had half a worm on it, so I just bent the limb down in the water and the fish grabbed the hook.

I let go of the limb and it came up with the fish. I grabbed the line and threw the fish over on the bank. It came off the hook, but I managed to kick it away from the water. That was the first steelhead I caught in my life, and it was the biggest fish I caught up to that point in my life. The only other steelhead I've caught, I got in the ocean.

We used to go swimming at Englishman River Falls and one of the holes was always full of steelhead. We tried to catch them with salmon roe, minnows and everything else, but it was summer time and they wouldn't bite. I was talking to Albert Sutton and told him about these fish.

"Oh," he said to me. "Get one of your Mom's sealers. Get a quart sealer. Put a bunch of sand in it. Go down to Ernie Johnson's and get some carbide and put it in there, put a bit of water in it and throw it in the water, but make sure you put enough sand in so that it will sink down amongst those fish and explode. You go downstream in the shallow water and pick them up when they float down, as it will stun them."

We did like he told us and got a sealer rigged up. Fred and Reg ran down stream and I put it in the pool. It blew off and five of the steelhead came floating down through the rapids to where Fred and Reg were. They managed to get three of them. We knew it would not be a good idea to get caught doing that. We never did get caught, but it was interesting.

At the old company farms in the Malaspina College area, there was a caretaker whose name was Bill Richards. He had two children: Gwen, who was a great friend of my sister Marge, and Chev, who was a great friend of us boys. We used to stay overnight up at the Richards place at times, myself, Fred and Reg, and Gwen used to stay down at our place.

Chev and I woke up one morning, looked out the window and there were a bunch of pheasants in Bill Richards' back yard. We went and organized him and told him, "Come on." He was kind of hung over this morning, but he got his shotgun. The pheasants were out in his garden, just outside two French doors. He had just laid a beautiful, brand-new oak floor in his dining room. I opened the doors for him so he could shoot. I don't know what he was doing, but before he got to point the gun it went off and shot a great big ripper right in his brand-new floor. All the birds flew away. It's these kind of events in a kid's mind that stick in the memory.

2

IN 1939, THE SUMMER I TURNED FOURTEEN, big changes occurred in my life. The war started at the end of that summer, but even earlier I took the first steps from being a kid to becoming an adult. That summer I worked at Lake & Sons in Nanaimo. It was a little boat building shop, making clinker built boats and putting Briggs & Stratton engines in them. I worked there two summers for $1.00 a day, an amount which most people wouldn't consider working for. But it was a very interesting job for me, because of what I had learned from my dad about woodworking. I managed to get a set of patterns off the boats as we finished them, and eventually built four at home.

Also, that summer, I became the chief gunner in the Dorman family. We did a lot of night hunting with our farmer friend at Errington, Mr. Taylor, who still had a pit-lamping permit. I didn't get near as excited as my father when taking aim at a deer. He used to miss quite often. That year, when I turned fourteen, I shot fourteen deer with fourteen shots.

During that same year I had a *Vancouver Sun* paper route around Harewood. My dad had an old single-barrel shotgun that could be broken down. It was a 12-gauge that I could take apart and put in my newspaper bag. In the afternoons, when I delivered my papers, I was always running into pheasants. There were all kinds of them around Five Acres at the time. I would come home with pheasants more often than not. I always told my mom I got them with my BB gun. My dad probably knew what I got them with, because quite a few of them had a lot of pellets in them. But he never said anything.

Up behind Harewood was a huge farm that the Bebans farmed for Canadian Colliers, the old coal mining company. When I was a kid we often went up there to see all the animals— the cows, pigs, horses and so on. All of the old donkeys they used to use in the mines were up there. These poor old donkeys were blind from spending all their lives working underground, and they would walk into the fences.

In the spring thousands of band-tailed pigeons and geese would appear and eat the seeds when they were trying to put the crops in. In the fall the farm was a big stop-over for geese and ducks. Where those birds go now, I don't know, but they don't come around here any more.

After the war started, sometime in late 1939, an army camp was set up at the farm. When the war started in September, they put tents up and eventually it became a huge army base—we used to call it Nanaimo Army Camp. They built a hospital later, and a lot of huts. It was strictly a tent camp right through the first winter. In 1940 most of the buildings were built. I think at one time there were about 10,000 soldiers up there.

There were only two or three houses in that area; it was mostly open fields. As part of their exercises they would fly over with small planes, Cessnas, I think, and throw flour sacks at the soldiers.

The hydro people had just put up a big power line on Harewood Road, behind Harewood School, which is still there today. One afternoon, just after school, my brother Reg, Jack Holsey and Bill Forrester were watching these guys in the plane throw flour sacks at the soldiers in the field. The plane clipped the top wire of the power line with a wheel and broke it. The plane just about crashed and the wire came down and hit a bike my brother and his friends had. Those are high powered wires. It burnt the bike and Holsey got the worst of it. He was in shock for quite a few years after this accident, before he really came around to forgetting about it. Reg and the other guy were lucky that they weren't electrocuted. They didn't get under the wires again, I can tell you that.

While we lived on Five Acres there were a lot of men from the neighbourhood who went into the war. A lot of them were real heroes, did a lot of great fighting, and won a lot of medals to boot. Some never did come back. I remember two of them, the Butler boys, who lived up on Wakesiah. They both went into the Air Force and were lost over Germany. There were quite a few more who died in the Army. A lot of them came back and most of them were great heroes to us kids.

Some of the soldiers at the camp had an old Model T that they parked behind Harewood School, on Harewood Road. One Sunday night Davy Peffers and I went up there and were looking at the car. He said, "How about you cranking; I'll see if I can get it going."

"We might get hell if we take this thing," I said.

"Oh, we'll just see if we can get it going."

"Okay."

While I was cranking it he pumped up and down on a lever. I guess it was a spark advance on the steering wheel. The thing backfired and sent me flying. My wrist swelled up like crazy. I knew I was going to get heck for this.

This was a Sunday night and every Sunday night we kids used to have a bath. It wasn't too often we had a bath in those years, because we didn't have the hot running water we have today. I came home, went upstairs, and didn't say a thing to my mother. The bathtub was upstairs, in the house on Fifth. I went up, got in the bathtub, and got washed. Then, Bang! Bang! I stomped my feet on the bottom of the tub. I started hollering and my mother came running up. "What's wrong?," she wanted to know.

"I slipped and fell in the bathtub and it looks like I broke my arm." The next day, I had to go to the doctor, Dr. McNeilly was his name. He sent me for X-rays. I had a broken wrist and it was put in a cast for about three or four weeks.

When my arm was almost better, I had another mishap. We used to have Soap Box Derbies in Nanaimo. Fred, Reg and I each had a car that we kept on the front veranda of the house. I went outside one dark night and tripped over one of those soap boxes. I fell down on that arm and thought I broke it again, but it was just swollen. The Soap Box races were a lot of fun. We used to go down Fitzwilliam Street, just coasting. We did that for quite a few years. and my brothers carried on after me when I left.

We used to sell newspapers up at the army camp. Fred and I sold the *Colonist* in the morning and the *Sun* in the afternoon, so we always had a little extra money. We had a great time selling newspapers, drinking milk shakes and getting tooth-aches from eating chocolate bars.

During this time we were still cutting firewood. After school and on weekends Fred and I would run or walk out to where we were working, way beyond the army camp. Later we got bikes and hid our tools up there.

Once, at Tea Swamp Hill, a steep hill just above the Nanaimo Fish and Game Club, Gogo's logging truck lost its brakes and went into the ditch. They were hauling four or five nice fir logs and they dumped them all. They lay there for a long time. Finally, Fred and I thought, "We'll cut these up." We were already cutting further up the road, and this wasn't so far to go. We cut them up into twelve-inch lengths for a fellow by the name of Percy Lisk. It took four ricks four feet high by eight feet long to make a cord. He used to pay us $2.25 a rick.

The Gogos weren't logging for some reason and we just about had the logs all sawn up before anyone noticed what we were doing. We were on the biggest one last, of course, and it was easy to split. It was a nice log, I think about twenty-seven inches through and thirty-odd feet long; a deadly peeler; straight grain. It split like nothing.

Mr. Gogo phoned up my dad one night and said, "George, I understand your boys have been sawing up my load of logs that was dumped up on Nanaimo Lakes Road at Tea Swamp Hill."

"Oh, have they now," my dad said. "I'll have to ask them." He asked us if we had been sawing up a load of logs on the hill.

"Yeah," I said. "They've been there for ages." So, he told Mr. Gogo we had.

"Well," he said. "I don't want a lot of money for those logs, George, but I should have at least five dollars for that load."

"Can the boys finish cutting it up and we'll give you the five dollars?"

"Oh, of course, they can cut it up and just give me the five dollars." That little load of logs, I would say, probably gave us about six cords of wood, for which we were getting $2.25 a rick, nine bucks a cord. So we got about $54.00. We had to do some work for nothing to pay for the logs, but we didn't mind at all. Those were the easiest logs we ever cut up.

When I was going to school in Harewood, I also played a lot of sports, softball and soccer, mainly, plus basketball and lacrosse. Even after the war years I kept up my lacrosse until I got into the sawmill business, and I continued to play soccer to about 1954. The other thing I did a lot of was running. I ran like a deer. I hardly weighed anything, 131 pounds when I joined the Navy. When I was in grade ten, I represented Harewood for most of the running sprints. I could really run the mile, or any distance that was long. I got lots of training running up and down the Nanaimo Lakes Road trying to find some firewood before I owned a bicycle.

When I turned sixteen in 1941 I started working, so I didn't see much of the farm in Errington any more. I missed that. I got work as a millwright at the Surret sawmill on South Forks road, near where the Gogo mill is today. The following summer, when I turned seventeen, it was easy to get a job in the sawmills because a lot of men were away at the war. In June of that year my pals were getting jobs in Port Alberni, for Bloedel, Stewart & Welch, or at Nanoose Sawmill. I went to Nanoose Bay and got myself hired at the mill for twenty-five cents an hour. I was to come to work on a Monday.

Mack Sebastion, who was superintendent at the Surret mill, heard about me being a half-assed carpenter, so he offered me a job at forty-five cents an hour. I thought, "Oh, this is great!" after my dollar-a-day boat building job. I didn't work at all at Nanoose, but instead went to Surret's.

When I went to work I took my little box of tools with me—hammers, saws and so forth. They were building big sawdust bunkers and wood bunkers. My first job was making doors for the bunkers. After I got them built and put up, I helped build a big bridge across Boulder Creek, which was really something for me.

It had six bents made of twenty-foot posts, on twenty-foot centers. Across the top of each bent we put a crosspiece, and on them, five great big logs. We broadaxed them flat on top and then put some eight-by-eights across them. On these we laid four-by-twelve planks, with ten-by-ten guard rails. When we got this bridge built, man, were we happy. On the Labour Day weekend, after we had been using the bridge for a week, they decided to burn some slash. They got a fire started early in the morning, and it took no time at all to get away from them. By 3:30 in the afternoon it had burned our new bridge, and by 5:30 the mill went up in flames.

There were quite a few of us guys there. The Chinese fallers had long since fled when they heard about the fire coming. Then the road got cut off and we couldn't get back out onto the South Forks Road. The road to Nanaimo Lakes wasn't there at that time. We went down to the old Chinese shacks and waited there for quite some time. I couldn't believe the number of deer coming out of the fire. The deer would run out and then go back into the trees where the fire was. The blue grouse would fly out of the fire and back into it again, too. There were so many animals around there at that time, and it was hard to believe they would be that stupid.

There were twenty-two of us and we got to the Chinese shacks an hour or so before dark. One of the older fellows, Andy Hunter, had a single-barrel shotgun. We were dirty, messy and hungry, so I said, "Andy, how about getting me your shotgun. I'm going to go underneath the cabin and shoot some of the chickens under there."

But Andy decided he wanted to have the fun. "I'll go shoot the chickens; you peel the potatoes." The Chinamen had left some potatoes and onions. Andy went underneath the cabin and shot a couple of times. Everybody was trying to get the hell out of the way. I was peeling the potatoes at the sink and, POW! There were potatoes flying up in my kisser. I don't know what Andy did but his gun went off and blew a big hole up through my potatoes, and into the ceiling. God, we were spitting out pellets half the night after we ate those potatoes. That was my first near miss, but we all had a good laugh.

Before long it got so smoky we decided we had to get out of there. We crossed the Nanaimo River and we walked down through the mill's timber holdings and along some old logging roads to Cassidy. We arrived there in the morning, twenty-two hours after the fire got away. We all survived, but neither the sawmill nor the bridge did.

After the weekend I went back to school, into grade eleven. The first weekend, on Friday night, my dad said "Come on, get your bags packed and we'll go to the cabin in Errington."

"Father," I said. "I'm not going up to the cabin this weekend, and I am not going back to school on Monday. I am going to work." With that he hauled off and gave me a punch in the head. My relationship with my father after that, I will have to admit, was very poor. He barely spoke to me for about ten years.

I went and got my job back with the Surrets. They decided they were going to build another sawmill so they got hold of a fellow by the name of Williams, who had a little business in Parksville. He used to cut planks for the logging roads up in the Errington area. He told the Surrets about a sawmill at Fanny Bay, built by a fellow by the name of Tanksky. He had finished the mill, which was in a nice, huge building made out of hemlock timbers. He had a bunch of people in to show them his new sawmill. He was showing them how the edger worked. It had an electric eye to open and close the rollers. He stuck his head into the edger and a roller came past the electric eye. The rollers closed on his head and made hamburger out of it. That's why the mill went up for sale before it ever had lumber piled up in the yard.

I went up there with Williams and Neil Moore to take this sawmill apart. We brought it down to the new mill site, called Eureka Sawmill, where CIPA Lumber is now. We got smoke stacks and boilers from the Mayo mill in Duncan, and that's when I met a fellow by the name of Fred Davidson, who did me a lot of good through my life and helped me a lot. We worked together putting up the boilers, the high smoke stacks and such. I got all the high jobs because I wasn't scared of heights.

We soon got the Eureka mill framed up. About the time

we finished, Mayo started to build another mill. This mill was built at McKay Lake, between Duncan and Nanaimo. I got in on the ground floor building that sawmill through Fred Davidson, and worked on it through the winter of 1942–43.

There were a lot of Chinamen working at Mayo's, and once they started producing lumber from the mill, in May, they had me building cabins for them to stay in. They were just boxes, with steep sloping roofs, just cabins with big central stoves in them. The Chinamen used to sit there by the hour after work, smoking opium or whatever they smoked in their water pipes every night. I got to be good friends of a lot of the Chinese workers. They were good to me and I built them lots of shelves and other things in their rooms. If I'd stayed there I would have learned a lot more Chinese.

After that job I started working in the mill, cutting lumber, and I began to learn head sawing. That was the first time I had anything to do with unions. They were forming a new union down in Honeymoon Bay, and they called it the IWW—I Won't Work. Those fellows used to come up and try and get us guys going. Two of the people who worked in Honeymoon Bay got two of their agitators working up in the Mayo mill. That union almost got in there, but in the end it failed. They were a bunch of Commies, and the IWA took over.

In my lunch hour, when I didn't have millwright work to do, I went down to the boom shack to eat my lunch. That lake was so full of trout, I used to get a lunch bucket full of trout every time. There were also a lot of grouse and deer around the lake, which it didn't take me long to start hunting.

At Mayo, I learned to be a sawyer. I started out working on the carriage, and in time I got to do most of the jobs all through that sawmill. That's where I got my first real good sawmilling experience, which paid off great dividends for me in the long run.

That summer we had a flash fire in the sawmill. There were two big carriage drive fibre frictions for pulling the carriage back and forth. They got heated up and caught fire. There were great big babbitt bearings in the saw arbours that were oil fed. Oil got down to the frictions, and I guess the heat set the whole thing on fire.

When this happened, my friend George Payne was walking past a big bucket of whitewash. One of the Chinamen had just mixed up this whitewash and was painting with it. George grabbed a fire bucket and threw all the whitewash onto the flames, but that didn't do much.

From end to end in that whole sawmill building there was dust up in the rafters. When the flames got up there, it took fire in one big puff. It was smouldering and burning here and there so I climbed up above the carriage with a small fire hose. Just then four Chinamen came running through the door with a four-inch hose. They didn't see me up there and blasted me right out of the rafters. I fell down onto a pile of logs. I never hurt myself, but I cursed those Chinamen something good. They all said they were sorry, and stood there grinning away.

We got the fire out and on our next pay cheque, Mr. Mayo gave us ten dollars each for saving his sawmill. I thought that was very nice of him. We had a little bit of repair work to do, as some of the wires were burnt, but we got the mill going in about a week.

From the start, at Mayo, I was always looking for a chance to be a sawyer. Sometimes the foreman, Bill Owen, needed somebody to work on the carriage and he would get me to do that, besides building the Chinese shacks and other things. The sawyer's name was Ray Vaganella, an old Nanaimo guy. That summer, when I was setting on the carriage, Bill Owen made a lot of trouble with Vaganella, so he let me saw for the last half hour or so almost every day.

One day he got up to let me saw, and the log on the carriage happened to be a big 41-foot white pine log—a lovely log. Mostly, white pine went to Scotland for pattern stocks in the foundries. We cut it into $1\frac{1}{4}$, $2\frac{1}{4}$ or $3\frac{1}{4}$ inch boards. The sap was running at the time and the log was real slippery. I got it on the carriage and cut off a $2\frac{1}{4}$ inch, then I cut off a $3\frac{1}{4}$, and another $3\frac{1}{4}$. It was still clear, and I thought I'd cut another one. I was almost into the heart of the log, and when I went to back up the carriage, the log slid out and rolled against the saw. I was smart enough to go ahead on it, not back up, because the teeth would have caught and that would have been the end of that arbour. We had quite a wrestling match to get that half-log back onto the carriage. There were enough guys around that we got it on. We backed up, changed the saw because there was a bit of a buckle in it, and cut up the log.

I didn't buckle many more saws after incident. It taught me a lesson. The sawyer had taken off out of the mill instead of standing around and giving me some advice, which he should have done. That never happened to me again. That's where I first got to know a little bit about the sawing business.

After that, I got to be a fair sawyer, and I got a little more respect. All the guys liked me and I got to run the saw when Vaganella didn't want to come out on Saturdays. I remember one Saturday, we had some ties to get out for a ship out of Chemainus. They were six-by-eights and were going to China. That day I cut 25,000 board feet in one day. I thought that was quite a thing for me to be able to do, and I guess the other guys did too because they were all happy with me.

One of the other chores I had was to take all the cull logs, stain and conk mainly, and saw them into four-by-fives. They used to go for lagging for the #8 Mine that adjoined the mill property. One of my jobs was to drive the truck and, with a couple of helpers, get all the laggings to the mine. Jess Good, who turned out to be a great friend of mine in later years, was the foreman there. He took me down in the mine, and that was the only coal mine I was ever in. I didn't think it was the kind of a job I would like to have.

At that mill one of the things we cut a lot of when they had real good fir, was six-by-twelve and wider; it went to Australia. I got into that business myself years later. Between Hillcrest Lumber and Mayo Lumber it was a toss up as to who had the best wood, and who cut it the best. They were both outdoing Chemainus, which was really something at that time.

In September of 1943, I knew I had to make up my mind about going into the army or joining one of the other services. At first I decided to join the air force, and I guess I'm lucky I didn't get in there because most of my pals who did never made it home. I had to wait six months, and while I was waiting my eighteenth birthday came up, so I decided I had better not wait around any longer or the army would have got me.

One day six of us—a couple were from Chemainus, one

from Ladysmith and the other three from Nanaimo—decided to join up. A fellow by the name of Jack Hackwood borrowed his uncle's new Chrysler and we went off to Victoria like we were going to win the war. Jack was a hot shot fellow who used to have a little meat market on Haliburton Street. My mom used to buy all her meat from him, and he delivered it in a little Austin.

We were going down to Victoria and we all said, "Give 'er, Jack!" and that was the first time I ever went 100 miles an hour in a car. It was a big car, but we would have been all dead if we'd hit anything. When we got to Victoria we signed up for the navy, and went home to wait until we were called up.

While I was waiting, I had sex for the first time in my life. I met this girl in Nanaimo, a gorgeous girl, through a friend of mine and phoned her one Sunday morning about ten o'clock. I asked her what she was doing and she said "Nothing."

"I'll come down and see you," I said.

"Have you got a couple of bottles of beer?"

I said I did. "When can I come?"

"Whenever you wish," she said.

At that time I didn't have any wheels, only my bicycle. I was still living at Harewood so I rode my bike all the way down to the south end of Nanaimo. I met her and we drank the beer. We had a deadly sex party. The first time I had a climax it felt like a flock of pigeons flying up my backside. I thought, this is great. It sure beat the hand jobs I'd been using previously.

After a while I thought maybe we should try this again. We did and, again, it was just great. The girl moved away from Nanaimo and I never saw her again. But I can still see her big, smiling, happy face, with the nicest teeth. She enjoyed the sex greatly and I guess that kind of set me onto my sex drive.

Through the years, and four marriages, I got a little experience with girls, the good, bad and the ugly. I'll tell you one thing: All girls aren't the same. Some are real sex pots and some are not, but they're still a lot of fun.

George Dorman,
age 4, with his
first wagon, in
Vancouver.

The Dorman
family in 1929 at
their Vancouver
house. (Front to
back) Reg, Fred,
George,
Dorothy, Marge,
Gertrude and
George Sr.

Harewood Public School class picture, 1933. George Dorman is in middle row, the big kid with the cowlick. His pal Dave Peffers is on his right.

The Dorman boys in Vancouver, 1928. Reg (l), George and Fred.

The late George (Pop) Dorman with two of his famous inlaid cribbage boxes. Mr. Dorman estimated he had produced more than 5,000 of the crib boards during his lifetime. Most were given away to friends or visitors.

Alf Flett photo. If you have old photographs of Nanaimo or district people, events or places of interest, we would be pleased to publish them, with as much detail as possible, in our Remember When? series.

George Dorman Senior, remembered in a recent *Nanaimo Daily Free Press*.

A Buck & Turner logging truck, with cheeseblocks, broke down on Wakesiah Avenue in 1935.

At the opening of the Golden Gate Bridge in San Francisco, 1935.

The yard of the Harewood house in 1936. Dorothy Dorman (l),
Fred, Art Dorman, a cousin from Bowen Island in rear, George and
Butch Branchini. The Dorman family's 1934 Essex is at right.

Albert Sutton with his Wee McGregor drag saw at Nanoose in
1936, with the Dorman boys. George (l), Fred and Reg.

The cabin at Errington under construction . . .

. . . and finished, 1937.

Fred Dorman, age 8,
at Departure Bay with
the first salmon
George caught.

George Dorman, age 14, and his father with a five-point buck
George shot as it walked along a log at Errington in 1939.

George Dorman, senior and junior, at Harewood house, Nanaimo
1947. Four-point buck on ground weighed 184 pounds.

The Five Acres area of Nanaimo in 1938, from the Dorman kitchen
window. The fields in the background were part of the Canadian
Colliers farm, the one on the right the present site of Malaspina
College.

George Dorman
at Nanaimo in
1943, just after
18th birthday,
before going into
Navy.

George Dorman
in Navy, St.
Johns,
Newfoundland,
1945.

The swimming WREN with Jack Cowan, who retired at White Rock and died in 1991. Shelburne, Nova Scotia, 1945.

George Dorman at Shelburne, Nova Scotia, 1945.

Opposite page: Two photos found by George Dorman aboard the German U-Boat U190 when it was captured off Newfoundland in 1945. Top: The U190 being commissioned in Germany. Bottom: The pipe along conning tower is part of a new underwater breathing apparatus. The periscope of this submarine is now in the St. Johns Legion hall.

George Dorman (l) and Johnnie Bohoslowich on Newcastle Island
in 1946.

3

WHEN I WENT INTO THE NAVY, in March of 1944, I took my training in Vancouver on the *HMS Discovery*, which I think had just opened around that time. While I was there I met a set of twin sisters. There was no sex involved. I would date one or the other of them, but I was never sure which girl I was with half the time. I think that more than once they played tricks on me and I was going out with both of them. The same thing happened to me in Ladysmith once, with another set of twins, although that time I'm pretty sure I always went out with the same one.

After I finished my training I worked on the base for a couple of months, waiting to go to Toronto. I worked on my own and had to report in the morning and at night, but I couldn't leave the base.

Part way through the summer I met a girl who was a great sex pot. One day I was doing some work on the dock and she came along in a little row boat. She was a Swede who had the greatest sun tan. You couldn't think of a better looking girl, long blonde hair. She lived on her father's fish boat, which was tied up across from *HMS Discovery*, where the Bayshore is today.

She would come over in her row boat and get me. I'd lay in the bottom of the boat and she'd row over to her dad's fish boat. He was away somewhere. We'd have a nice love in, then she'd row me back to the base. Her father always had liquor on board the boat. He was always good to sailors. I met him on occasion. That romance only lasted a couple of weeks, and then I got shipped to Toronto.

I was sent to classes at Brunswick University for six or seven months to learn to be a shipwright. The classes started at 3:30 in the afternoon and went until 10:30. During the day the University was being used by other people.

At first we were staying in barracks at the Canadian National Exhibition grounds down on the lake. After we lived in the barracks for a while there were so many soldiers, sailors and airmen in there we had to move out, and went to live in town. We called it lodge and scrounge, because we had to scrounge for our meals. They gave us enough money to pay for the room, and that was about the size of it. We didn't get boarded, it just covered rent for the room. We lived out and went to university for another six or seven months.

Right next to the University there was a beer parlour and hotel, the Brunswick House. I got to know a guy in there. He wasn't from the military because he was 4-F. He was a real good guy and he talked me into seeing if I could get him some booze. I only drank beer at that time, but I scrounged around and finished up with about five liquor licences. There were a lot of guys in our gang that didn't drink. I didn't tell them what I was doing with the liquor.

We were allowed was one bottle of liquor a month on a licence. When you bought a bottle the guy in the liquor store stamped the back of the card. I carried a little bottle of fingernail polish remover and, every time I got a card stamped, I wiped it off and went on to another liquor store. I used to buy the booze for about $2.40 or $2.45 and my friend paid me $7.00 a bottle. Also, I bought a bottle from other guys for $5.00, and sold it for $7.00. I ended up with a nice little bootlegging business, and made myself a good profit. We were only paid thirty-three dollars a month, so with my bootlegging income I was able to more than feed myself.

In Toronto I had any amount of encounters with girls. One of the funniest was when I met a sixteen-year-old at a party. She was with her sister, who took off with another sailor. We partied most of the night and afterwards we were walking home to her house. We stopped in a park, to have sex on a bench.

Just as we were getting into it there was a tap, tap on my shoulder. An old guy said to me, "Hey, can't you find someplace else to do this?"

"No," I said. "I don't have a home, I've got no place else. Why don't you go sit down?'

"Okay," he said. "Do you mind if I watch?"

"I don't care." I went on with my little diddle and walked the girl home. The guy was still sitting there with his little old wife. They must have both been eighty years old.

About two weeks later, I was with the same girl. Her parents had a place over on Center Island. They went over there with their son and left the two sisters at home. We had a big party at their house one night. We couldn't get anything very good to drink, and I'd been drinking wine, which, along with beer was most affordable. I was barfing out the second story window and did a loop out into the yard. I landed in a rhododendron bush and didn't hurt myself, but my back was a little sore for a couple of days.

This girl's brother had a tent pitched in the back yard. That night, her sister was with my pal in the house. We were in this tent having a little fun. At about four o'clock in the morning there was a flashlight shining in my face and someone was kicking me.

"What the hell are you doing?" I asked the guy.

"I'm the police. Come out here, I want to talk to you." I got out of the sleeping bag.

"What do you know about this?" he asked me. Next to the yard was a liquor store, and behind us, thirty feet away, was a great big hole through the bricks in the side of the building. Somebody had made a hole and ran off with a whole load of booze. We hadn't heard a thing. When you've had good sex you sleep well—a lot more people should realize that.

There were thirty-nine of us fellows in my company at Brunswick University, and we were from all over Canada. Most of the guys had been car knockers, working in the railroad yards as repair men, so they had some woodworking and metalworking experience, which I had also. That's how we all were grouped together, and stayed together for quite some time after leaving Toronto.

The summer of 1944 was super hot. It was nice to be able to go to school at night because it would give us all day to swim. We did a lot of swimming in the lake and had a lot of fun even though we got thrown out of a couple of places.

That summer I met two sisters from Oshawa. They had a friend, so myself and a couple of pals from Nanaimo went to a party they had for us in Oshawa. They had cars and picked us up. We had a pass and went for the weekend. They were married and their husbands were in the airforce. I heard later they were all killed overseas.

We had a great party. Most people won't believe this, but between nine o'clock that night and ten the next morning that girl and I had sex ten times. The last time we were down at the lake, swimming. There was a training place for the air force there, where they were flying Harvards. These guys were flying over us at about fifty feet, watching us.

When we moved out of the barracks, three of us rented a single room in a rooming house near the Brunswick House. Two of us would take turns going for walks with our girls, while the other one had sex in the room. That was one of the only times in Toronto I had a good bed to have sex in.

The landlady lived in this big, two-storey house all by herself. One night when I came home the landlady wasn't there. Upstairs we had a big, old bath tub and me and one of my pals filled it full of beer. We had some girls coming to see us, so we were going to have some fun. There were quite a few of us in on all that beer at our party. By the time the landlady came back, we were kind of noisy so she told me we had to find another place to stay. I tried to talk her out of it, but she wouldn't change her mind.

The next day, we had to go off somewhere and when we came back to go to school we found all our bags thrown out on the lawn. Across the road and there was a big sign on the house, ROOMS FOR RENT, so we went over and talked to that lady. Oh yeah, sure, she will take us in. We moved into that place and party time was on most nights, especially on weekends.

In the meantime, the lady across the road phoned the navy out at the base and told them us fellows were too rowdy. She had kicked us out and now we were living across the street, keeping her awake. We got collared into living back in the barracks, which wasn't much fun, but at least we had a little more money left over.

In the winter of 1944, when we back in the barracks, there was a huge snow storm. For three days we could not get in or out of the barracks. It was the worst snow storm I ever saw. The exhibition buildings had windows twenty or twenty-five feet high; they were high buildings. The snow was up to the top of the windows on the windward side where the drifts blew up.

One of the good things about being back in the barracks was that there was a workshop there where I could make things to sell, and make a bit of extra money. I built a model of the Bluenose, six feet long. I made all the boards and planks, just like the original boat was built, out of little pieces of wood. Today it's in Ottawa, somewhere in one of the navy buildings there. They have it in a little glass case with my picture and a name plate beside it. That was quite a feat. It took me three months to make that, as well as do all my written, welding and metal work. It kept me quite busy.

Later on, I built a fancy lamp for my girl friend. An officer by the name of Simon wanted this lamp in the worst way, and he said to me, "Hey, George, that girlfriend of yours can't make you a fourth class officer but I can. You better give me the lamp if you want to be a fourth class officer."

"I promised her this lamp," I said, "and I'm not giving it to you. If my ability isn't good enough to become a fourth class officer then you don't have to give it to me."

Out of the thirty-nine of us he gave one guy, who was thirty-five years old, a fourth class and the rest of us all got fifth class. That was another bit of extra money you got every month but I didn't let it bother me because I knew the war was coming to an end. I think about that officer quite often, and I don't know where the lamp is today.

In January, 1945, we packed up in Toronto and headed off to Newfoundland. We caught the train and went first to Halifax.

We were there about two or three weeks, waiting for a convoy to go to Newfoundland.

There weren't many girls in Halifax, and no sex. There were so many sailors you couldn't find a girl to save your butt. They had beer there that was just as green as you could ever imagine, and we used to say it was made of either French safes or boxing gloves because every night after drinking it the fellows ended up fighting. This was because there were no girls.

One of the things I did in Halifax was win beer. I only weighed 131½ pounds. I would tap dance on the table and bet the fellows I could put my hands right around my whole waist. I was the only guy who could ever do that.

I was able to do it for almost a year. And after that, forget it; look at me today—it takes ten hands to go around my middle.

Finally, we caught a convoy out of Halifax to Newfoundland. We were on a troop ship with 5,400 sailors, air force and army guys on board. They were replacements for the different services overseas. The weather was just awful. It was the beginning of February by this time, and the waves were super high. These fellows were sick, laying all over the place, and it was the biggest mess you ever saw. All my pals from the Brunswick University were on board, and all of them were sick.

I had to do four hours on and four hours off. They put me up on a gun opposite the bridge, a single 20-millimetre Oerlikan gun. I got to take a few whaps with it to make sure it was working. The gun kind of hung out the side of the ship in a turret. To get to it I had to wait for the ship to roll to the right, then I'd run up the ladder and go head first into this thing. We had radio contact to the bridge. There were thirty-three merchant ships in the convoy and it took a few days to get to Newfoundland. At night there was a lot of activity with U-boats or something, I don't know for sure. During the night, and sometimes during the day, they were dropping depth charges. There was often a lot of noise out there and I always wondered what was going to happen next.

On our four hours off, they were always looking for volunteers to peel potatoes, so I used to go way down in the hold of the ship and peel potatoes. I didn't tell the guys until after we got to Newfoundland. They said, "How come, you suckholing bastard Dorman, you were down there peeling potatoes all the bloody time."

"It was better than sitting up there with you guys barfing all over the place," I said. "If you get in the bottom of the ship, in the center of the ship where the potatoes were, you wouldn't get seasick." That's one of the reasons why I never ever got seasick.

The very first night I was in Newfoundland I went to a roller rink. I ran into two friends of mine from Nanaimo named Dave Peffers and Ted Jinkison. They introduced me to a girl and I took her home that night. Her mother was already in bed, upstairs, so we went into the living room. We had a little rattle against the post at the bottom of the staircase leading upstairs. When she climaxed she fainted. I couldn't figure out what happened to her. I took her over and put her on the chesterfield. She finally came around and we talked for a bit.

We had sex on a few more occasions, and every time she had a climax she fainted. One night, just after we had sex on the chesterfield, her mother came out of the kitchen to ask us if we wanted some tea. I said that would be great. She asked if her daughter wanted some. I said she was sleeping, just leave her be. By this time I was starting to think I'd had enough of this relationship so I cleared out.

When we arrived in Newfoundland we had to stay up in the barracks and sleep in our hammocks. It was cold, but it wasn't too bad. Every day we had to march down those steep St. Johns streets to the shipyards and work on the ships that came in off convoys. They would stop here and all the boys would bail off. They didn't have much turnaround time, and then they had to go out on the next convoy.

Those ships, after going through the Atlantic in winter, came in so top heavy with ice I was surprised some of them didn't turn turtle. The ice had to be steamed off, but that wasn't our job; that was seamens' job. We were shipwrights and our job was to repair the damage to these ships from waves coming over and banging things up.

One time I remember well was when myself and another fellow were fixing the doors on a locker. The hinges were broken, and we couldn't find somebody to get a key to open the door so we could weld it. I said to the other guy, "Oh, we'll just weld the goddamn thing. We'll just weld it right where it is. I'll hold it in place and you get welding."

While we were welding away there, an officer came up and asked, "What are you guys doing?"

"We're welding up this hinge," I told him.

"That compartment is full of hedgehogs." Hedgehogs were explosives, electrically fired off the bow of the ship at submarines. They were all set in the locker, with an explosive charge on the end. This locker was right full of spare hedgehogs. He managed to get a key and we got it open and did the thing properly—shielded the hedgehogs from what we were doing with our welding torch. That brought quite a few laughs from the boys.

In St. Johns harbour there was a pipeline for pumping fuel oil to the ships. They had steam pipes to heat the oil so it would flow easily. There were big boxes up the hill along the pipe and they were nice and warm inside. I was doing some guard duty up there one time in the winter, checking on the pipes. I came to one of these steam boxes and heard some girls' voices inside. I opened the door and shone my light into it. There were two girls living in there.

I talked to them a bit and they wanted to know if I'd like some sex. So I had sex with one of them, while the other one watched. Afterwards I thought, Uh oh, I should be using a condom. Every sailor in town's been screwing these girls. I got outside and there was about eight inches of snow on the ground. I peed in my hand and got handfuls of snow and washed myself. I never did get the clap, and I never did during all my years in the navy or at any time since.

Later in the year, the ships came through the ice packs coming down from the North Atlantic, and after cutting through all the ice there was no paint left on the bows or along the sides. They were shinied up, shiny as a new nickel after running through all those ice floes. It was really something to see.

While we were there, a friend of mine that I had met earlier in the navy in Vancouver who was a seaman was on guard duty was playing with his gun one day and blew off half his foot. He finished up down in Duncan as a barber. I see him now and again when I go that way.

There were huge shops at the shipyard and myself and my friend were charge hands, so we had access to them. We had a bit of time now and again while we were on duty, and we could get down there at night if we wanted to. We used to make knives and suitcases. When we made the knives we found some tool steel to make a nice five or six inch blade. We got old radio cases or galley dishes made of bakelite in different colours. We'd cut off rings of it and put them on the handles. We'd screw on a nut and put a fancy end on it, then grind it all up. It made a great looking knife. All the sailors wanted to have a knife, so we'd sell one to them for five bucks. They'd grab that knife for five bucks in just a minute and thought it was just the greatest, and I guess they were at that time because nobody else had any knives and we didn't get issued any.

They other thing we did a lot of was to make suitcases. The bottom and top of these suitcases were made out of pressboard, which there is lots of today, but at that time pressboard was something new. A lot of guys couldn't get all their stuff in their duffle bag, so they'd buy one of these suitcases. We used to sell them for five dollars, too. It was great to make a bit of money in our spare time, instead of sitting around drinking beer in the canteens. Making things in the shop for yourself, or to sell, was called "making rabbits," and it was frowned upon. Some of the officers knew I was doing it, and asked me to make things for them, so I never got in trouble over it.

One day we were working across the harbour from St. Johns, up in the hills, an area called Dogpatch. There were oil tanks up there with pipes to get the oil down to the ships.

We were working over there one day on a ship and one of the hot shot pilots they were sending back to Canada to train others flew in. He had spent a lot of time in the war theatre over Germany as a fighter pilot. He was showing off doing spins and stalls, and came along upside down in the harbour, which was a very constricted area for upside-down flying. When he pulled the plane up it was too late and he crashed into the side hill, just missing all the big eight-inch oil pipelines. I was the first guy up to that airplane and it was smashed all to hell. The poor guy was fried, so he didn't get to train any Canadians. I guess guys get to be a little reckless now and again, especially in war years, because war itself is reckless.

In March 1945, Frank Sinatra came to Newfoundland to sing for the boys and entertain the troops. I had a friend by the name of Ink Pen who managed to get a bottle of rum. He called it "Newfie Screech." He and I drank that bottle of rum, and I guess I drank more than he did.

When it came time to go and see Frank, he and I were loaded. All the guys left and we thought we had better have a shower and get over there. So, Ink Pen and I had a shower. He took off to dress, and left me sitting on the floor of the shower, with the cold water coming down on me. He came back, all dressed, and said, "Let's go."

"Yeah, why not? Let's go." I came out of the shower, turned it off and headed for the door to go down the stairs.

"Hey, you've got to get dressed." he said.

"Oh, I'll go over there and give Frankie a treat."

"Hey, Dorman," he said. "You're going to get shit for this."

"Oh well, whatever you think." In the door we go. There were some MPs inside the door, two of them. They saw me bare balls and tried to grab me. I booted it down the aisle. Old Frankie's up there singing away up on the stage, and that hall was jammed, about a third of them Wrens. I streaked right down the aisle to Frankie and said, "Hey, Frankie boy, here I am. My name is George. Good to meet you."

By this time I had two or three of the MPs behind me. They grabbed me and back I went to the barracks. They made me get dressed, and down to the digger I went.

I got two weeks in the digger, and when you got in the digger you had to do some work around the barracks, mainly clean out the showers and bathrooms. While I was doing this, it was the coldest time of the year and the boys were working down on the ships, just freezing to death. "Hey, Dorman, how are you making out?" they wanted to know.

"Oh, I get out every day to clean up the bathrooms and all

this stuff, and you guys are freezing to death down on the bloody shipyard working on the ships. I'm in the barracks and it's about eighty degrees. I'm having a howl, you guys, so keep on down there, you're doing a good job. In the meantime, I don't think you miss me do you?"

"No, we don't, but we miss the bullshit." By the time my two weeks were up most of the cold weather was over.

We kept on working on the ships and the weather was getting better. Everybody was getting a little excited because the war was coming to an end. The day before VE Day, we were instrumental in capturing the German submarine *U190* off Newfoundland. We didn't capture it; it surrendered. It was one of the latest German submarines, fitted with a snorkel so it could breathe underwater with the diesel engines running and charge the batteries without showing the conning tower. It was very heavily armed.

When we boarded it, I was one of the first people down the conning tower, and I have a lot of pictures taken between the time it was commissioned in Germany until it surrendered. Today the periscope of that submarine is in the Royal Canadian Legion in Saint Johns.

When VE Day took place in May we had a huge parade, with over 10,000 people. We didn't have to be at the parade if we didn't want to, but they checked the barracks to see where we were. Myself and some other guys decided not to go to the parade. We hid up in the attic in the building and an officer came up to go through the barracks to make sure all our hammocks were tied up and put away. He was just about to leave when one of the guys in the attic moved and fell between the joists. He came down through the ceiling onto the floor and broke his arm. The officers checked to see who else was up there, so we all got caught. In the end we didn't get in much trouble for it, but we got a good lacing down and we finished up out at the parade.

When the war in Europe ended they were after us to sign on to fight in the Pacific. They sent out forms to join the Americans and fight the Japanese, so all the guys in our company signed up, 100 percent, to go off to fight in the war against the Japanese.

Half of the company went off on a cruiser, the *Uganda*, to Australia and got torpedoed on the way. They all survived.

The rest of us stayed on in Newfoundland and after VE Day we started to demobilize some of the ships. Then they decided they were going to take us over to Shelburne, Nova Scotia. There were fourteen or fifteen of us who got on the corvette, *Athol*, and went to Halifax. On the way between Newfoundland and Halifax we threw overboard all the depth charges (without exploding them), all the bullets for the 4.5 inch navy gun, .303 bullets 'til hell wouldn't have it, guns, sten guns, and any amount of other war equipment. Over the side it went. By the time we got close to Halifax, that corvette was like a cork in the water.

We had bad weather coming into Halifax, and I thought that ship was going to roll over. When you went out on deck you wore your rain clothes and a big belt. There were lines hanging down off a cable that ran from bow to stern with rings on them. You hooked a ring into your belt to keep from getting washed overboard. I remember going out there and my feet were completely off the deck. I was hanging off that wire by my belt when a big wave came over. I thought that thing was going to tip over for sure, but we made it.

The Shelburne base had belonged to the air force at one time. They had Catalinas flying out from there on Atlantic patrol. Then they built a new base that allowed them to get further out into the Atlantic. The Shelburne base was then taken over by the navy. There were concrete runways into the water for the flying boats, and great barracks.

By the time we got there everything was starting to be demobilized. It was June, 1945, and there were all kinds of warships coming in, mostly frigates. My friend and I, who were charge hands, would pull these ships out of the water on the two ways, scrape the bottoms, and copper paint them. A lot of the ships were wracked quite badly along the keel and rivets had worked loose. We remounted these rivets because they were leaking. They were loose in the holes and we used to pop them out and put an oversize rivet in, which was quite a chore. We would have those ships up there for one to four days. I never knew they had so many frigates in the Canadian Navy, but when you have the third biggest Navy in the world, I guess you've got a lot of frigates and a lot of ships, period.

There was a stack of Wrens at Shelburne. I couldn't believe there were so many girls in the navy. The whole time I was there, I never left the base once. I had all kinds of girlfriends there. A guy didn't have to head up town looking for Shelburne girls. We just stayed on the base.

I had a relationship with a girl from Nova Scotia. She was a big, good looking girl with a nice bosom on her. We used to swim out and have sex while hanging on to the buoys they had anchored out there to tie the planes to. I guess her being a Bluenoser and me being a hot-blooded Pacific guy, we managed to hit it off in the water pretty good. It was better than anyplace else. Around the barracks it was pretty tough to try and have sex.

When I was a kid, before the war, and even after the war when I had time, we would swim from Departure Bay over to Newcastle Island. I always liked long-distance swimming, but I guess it helped wear out my legs, which were shot by the time I was sixty-five.

One day this girl and I swam across Shelburne Bay, which was ten or fifteen miles across. Seven of us started on the swim, but all the others turned back. On the other side some officers were having a party with a bunch of Wrens. One of them asked me where we came from and if we had passes. Of course, we didn't so he made us jump in the water and swim back across the Bay. We had to swim against the tide on the way back and it took us hours. I think I slept about eighteen hours after that, I was so tired. Everybody on the base was happy to see that we had made it. We didn't get into any trouble for leaving without going through the gate or for not having a pass.

There was a great bar in Shelburne which was run by a couple of big fellows and when I say big, these guys were big—tall not fat. The bar had to close around eleven o'clock at night. These guys used to carry on later with some of the girls. While we were there the two guys who ran the bar got in a fight over one of the Wrens, and one guy was killed. That went very bad against the other guy, but I never did find out what happened in the end because I left before it was all settled.

About two weeks after this killing, I was in there one night with my friend, Jack Cowan, from Saskatoon. He was older than I was, and was my enforcer. He was a big fellow, six foot four, and he weighed 240 pounds. We got in a lot of fights and if I didn't settle them he did. I used to do quite a bit of boxing at that time.

One night we were standing at a counter where you could get a hamburger or a hot dog, and got into a fight with some sailors. Half way down the bar a big, hot-headed Frenchman that I knew was drinking with his cronies. The Frenchman picked up one of the guys we were fighting with and slammed him against the wall. There was a coat hook on the wall and it went through the guy's neck and killed him.

The girls called the MPs and when they came running up I thought, "I'm not getting involved in this business. Let's get out of here." There was no back door out of the part of the bar we were in, so I did a header right through the window. It had little eight-by-ten-inch panes of glass. My pals came right behind me, and my big friend Jack just stepped through it, right out onto the ground.

The next day was Sunday and we didn't have to muster. We were just fiddling around the barracks when the phone rang. They wanted to know if George Dorman was there. The guys called me and I went to the phone. It was the officer of the day, and he said, "I want to talk to you."

"Okay, sir, when do you want to talk to me?"

"Well, I would like you to come right down if you would.", so I went to the Administration Building. He wanted to know what I knew about the fight. I told him what I saw.

"I understand you dove through the window in that building," he said.

"I can't lie about that. I did, sir."

"I just thought I would check as to whether you did or didn't, and you told the truth. Did you lose something as you were diving through that window?"

"No, sir," I answered.

"Might this be yours?" It was a watch my mother had given me. It had my name engraved on the back of it, along with my Navy number, V81679. "I thought you might want this back."

Oh, boy, I thought, I'm going to get into the glue here.

"We might want to call on you. I don't know whether you know it or not, but at the other end of that snack bar, one of those fellows was killed. Do you know the Frenchman?"

"Yes," I said. "I know him. He wrestled lots of times in the gym. I should know him, I think everybody knows him."

"Well," he said, "He's been charged. We might want to call on you. Away you go. Try and have a good day and don't lose your watch again. Thanks for telling the truth." I never forgot that—thanks for telling the truth.

In September we left Shelburne on a slow train to Vancouver, which took five days. I had gone back and forth three or four times in my navy years and I enjoyed riding the train. You could have a lot of fun on it. On one trip from Toronto to Halifax we got a bunch of beer and put it in the ice compartment of the big water cooler the old railway cars had. The conductor didn't care, we gave him a beer now and again, and we had cold beer all the way.

On this trip coming back, my pal and I were with some girls. One of the girls and I were having a little rattle under a blanket, and the *conduct*or wasn't too happy about our *conduct*.

After we got to Vancouver, they sent us to Esquimalt. They asked us if we wanted to stay in the navy for a while, demobilizing ships. By this time a lot of my pals were leaving. Some of them went to different bases near their homes, all across Canada. By the time we got to Esquimalt, there were only about four or five of us left out of the thirty-nine in our company.

At that time we had a pretty good commanding officer and he and I got along great. He was there when I did my streak for Frank Sinatra, although he wasn't our commanding officer at the time. He thought that was hilarious. "Dorman, they should have given you a medal instead of putting you in the digger for two weeks cleaning out the shit houses."

"Oh, well," I said. "I enjoyed cleaning out the shit houses. It beat being down on the dock with those frozen guys welding and working outdoors on those ships."

"Yeah, you're probably right there. Quite often things like

this happen and a guy is better off being in the digger than with what he was doing previously." He came to be a good friend.

When we were in Esquimalt he almost sucked me in. He had signed on for another year to be in command. He was a shipwright like ourselves, but he was up higher in rank and never did any work. He just liked to look around and tell us to do this or do that. He was just having a happy time.

Until the end of 1945 we worked demobilizing ships—taking guns off them, cutting here and welding there, generally tearing things apart and having a good time thinking about all the money we were going to make when we got out of the navy. At that time I was up to $53 or $54 a month in pay. Big deal! We started off at $31, and two years later here we were with such wages, but that's military. You fight for your country and most often the money you do get is just enough to have a few cigarettes, a few drinks, and a happy time. That's what it was all about, as who knew when he might be dead?

One night in December I couldn't get a pass to go out. We didn't have to stand watch any more and were more or less just employees. We were still sailors, but working just like employees tearing ships apart. I said to my pal Ink Pen, "Hey, I've got a hot date with a couple of girls. Do you want to come with me?"

"Yeah, why not? Sure, Dorman, I'll come."

"Hey," I said, "You'll love these girls, they're just great!"

There was a big wire fence around the base, with barbed wire like you see on the security fences along the top, so no one could get in or out. It was raining like crazy and I had my raincoat on. We climbed up the inside of the fence, and I was first, as usual. I was a little panicky. I think I was letting something run away with my brains at the time.

I got up to the top and jumped. My coat was much longer than Ink Pen's, and was hanging down. When I jumped, it caught up on the barbed wire. I went off that fence like a turkey, head down. My coat ripped and I fell to the ground, getting a sore wrist out of the deal.

I warned my friend, "Throw your coat over first." He threw his coat over the barbed wire crawled over it easily.

When we found the girls it was raining like hell, and we

had no place to go. By the time we managed to get over the fence it was 8:30. and the girls had to be home by 10:30. Our little romance didn't happen and we never saw those girls again.

When we came back we had to go back over the fence again. That wasn't easy. We found a spot where there was a pole near the fence, climbed up it, got over onto the barbed wire that was hanging out, and managed to get ourselves back into the barracks.

After that, we went on with our work every day, hoping we would soon get out. I wanted to get back working in a sawmill, making some good money. Finally at the end of January, 1946, we got out of the navy. Ink Pen went home to Edmonton, and the others went back to where they came from. I went home to Nanaimo and that was the end of the war for me.

4

BEFORE I WENT INTO THE NAVY, I had been working at the Mayo mill, so I went back there to work. They had to give me my job back, but there was no problem with that.

My first job was part-time sawing and working on the carriage. When they decided to build a big 400-foot long crane-way with a travelling crane on it, they asked me to help them build it. I had learned a lot from my friend, Fred Davidson, about building bents, bridges and sawmill buildings out of big timbers, so this crane-way was very simple. Fred had started out on this job but he had a bit of a drinking problem, and every time Mr. Mayo gave him shit he would quit. When I came along he had quit again and they had nobody to build the crane-way, so they asked me to do it.

We got a Cat in and cleaned up the area beside the sawmill. It was quite an uphill slope to the back on the 400-foot long crane-way. Since the top of it had to be level, the posts on the bottom bent were about thirty-six feet high. The whole thing consisted of about twenty of these bents, which were made of twelve-by-twelve posts, with crossbars between them. When we got all the bents up we were going to bolt twelve-by-sixteens along the posts, with tracks on them for the crane to run along. The crane was like a little bridge, and it moved up and down on tracks, picked up the lumber and put it in piles. When they wanted to load trucks they backed them in and the crane loaded the lumber on. We didn't have a proper method of doing things, and the operation was very amateurish. One day, after we had four or five bents up, I was climbing the posts with a plumb bob to make sure they were straight. The posts were temporarily braced with one-by-sixes, and I would climb them by nailing little sticks to them and climbing up on the sticks. On this occasion, when I was up the post, twenty-six feet off the ground, the fellow helping me tried to knock the braces off to straighten the post. He got one brace off, and the post started going over. I said to myself, "I'm gone off of here." I jumped onto a slope beside the crane-way, skidded down it, and lit on my chest. That knocked the wind out of me. When the post fell it knocked down four more of them. I couldn't get off the ground and I saw one coming at me, but I couldn't move because I was winded. It landed about three feet from me. If it had hit me it would have killed me. I was super upset. When I looked off in the distance, I saw my brother Fred, who was also working there, running toward me. He had a First Aid ticket. The boss, Bill Cannon, came over and said, "Holy Christ, Fred! Do we call a Doctor or an ambulance? Do you think your brother made it?" "Yeah, he made it," Fred answered. The only injuries I had were some bruised ribs and a cracked wrist. That was the only time I was ever off work in my whole life. I went back to work two weeks later.

In the spring of 1946, I had piles real bad so I went over to Shaughnessy Hospital in Vancouver and had an operation. They still had a lot of military doctors there at the time. Three days after my operation they told me to have a hot bath. Unbeknownst to me they had a bandage about twelve feet long up my rectum. When the doctor came, he had four or five other doctors with him. They were military doctors, left over from the war years, still learning. Anyway he got the bandage and yarded it out of there on three pulls. It hurt so much I thought I was passing razor blades, never mind just a bandage taken out. That same day a guy comes in and gets into the bed next to me. When I took a look at him I saw it was my long-time pal, Andy Poje. He had just had all his varicose veins stripped, which I think was as hard for him as my haemorrhoids were for me. We didn't have good doctors in those days.

During the summer of 1946 we had a bit of a fire season and Mayo shut the mill down. Johnnie Bohoslowich and I decided we were going to build a boat. I was still living at my Dad's house, on Machleary Street. We decided to build it, a twenty-two-foot clinker built boat, in the basement. As I mentioned, while I was working for Lake and Sons, before the war, I had made patterns for keels, stems, transoms, and so on. I got the lumber from Mayo's and we were set. When we started putting on the planks we found that the first four or five on either side of the keel had to be steamed to make them fit. After that they bent naturally without steaming them. For a steamer we took an old hot water tank, plugged the holes in it, and inserted a pipe to carry the steam to a wooden box. We put the hot water tank over a hole in the ground, filled it partly full of water, and lit a little fire under it to make steam.

After we steamed the last plank, we took it out of the steaming box and down to the basement to nail it on. I said, "Hey, Johnnie. Kick that thing over. We don't need it any more. " He did, but unknown to us, the pipe came out of the steam box and stuck in the ground. Part of the tank was still on the fire. While we were nailing the plank on, a neighbour, Victor Palmer, came over to ask us what the hell we were doing. He was a Spear & Jackson man that I met at Mayo's, who taught me how to hammer saws and who has been a business associate of mine over the years. "Are you getting in the jet age or something?" he asked. "Your hot water tank just lit in front of my lawn mower."

He lived on Pine Street and we were one street down, with an alley in between. When Johnnie kicked the tank over, because the pipe was stuck in the ground, it filled with steam and blew up. It flew clean over Victor's house and landed in front of him while he was mowing his lawn. I couldn't believe it until I went outside and saw the tank was gone. Johnnie and I went over to Victor's and, sure as hell, there was the tank sitting there. It was lucky somebody didn't get hurt.

When we finally got the boat finished, we decided to take it out of the basement and install the engine in the back yard. When we went to take it up the basement stairs it wouldn't go. It was catching on the floor. We thought about it and decided we had to take the concrete steps out. "I'll go down to Turley's," Johnnie said. Turley's was a rental place in those days. Johnnie went down with his truck and picked up a jack hammer. We took out the stairs and finally got the boat out. Then we rebuilt the stairs. We sold the boat to Percy Lisk, who bought firewood from us when we were younger.

In the winter of 1948-49, we lost a bit of work over snow and bad weather. I had the lumber so we decided to build a couple more boats. Johnnie and I built them in my house on Wakesiah, with Sam Sebastian and Andy Poje helping us towards the end for a small fee of about two dollars an hour.

We built the first boat and got it all painted and rigged up. We had the other one about half built, and decided to move it outside to put the engine in. We tried to get that boat out of the basement and, lo and behold, even though we had measured it up every which way, we could not get it up the stairs. So there we were, having to jack hammer the stairs again. Johnnie said, "That's my department. I'll go down to Turley's one more time."

We went through the whole procedure again and this time, when we cemented the stairs back in, we made sure we could get the other boat out, I can assure you of that. I built that boat out of yellow cedar for an old friend of mine, Frank Denton.

After we got the crane-way almost built at Mayo's I went back to sawing for J. Z. Miller, who needed a sawyer to run a little steam mill he had down on Michael Lake, near Cedar. The first morning I went there, all the saws were going. A fellow by the name of Cal Walker—who later was a writer for the *Nanaimo Daily Free Press*—was on the saw.

"What are you doing?" he wanted to know.

"I was hired to be the sawyer."

"Oh," he says, "I thought I was the sawyer."

"Well, they hired me, so you'd better go figure it out at the office. I'm going to be sawing." Off he went and I immediately started sawing the logs.

He came back over and said, "You know, nobody wanted this job."

"Why didn't anybody want the job?"

"This mill hasn't worked for a week," he said. "A plank flew off the saw here and killed a man that was turning logs. That's why they haven't got a sawyer."

"Well, I'm not going to let that bother me," I said. "I'm going to get on with it. I need the work."

When I took this job on, I got ninety cents an hour. Mr. Miller said to me, "If you can cut more than 18,000 feet a day, I'll give you a bonus of $175 a month." Great, I thought, that was more than half my wages.

Then he said, "If you cut more than 20,000 a day I'll give you $350 a month bonus." It didn't take me long to get 18,000, and before long I got over 20,000. I was making the best money around Nanaimo. It didn't happen without making a lot of people cranky with me, but I knew how to saw logs. With the speed of the carriage and the amount of steam available, we had a lot of power for a little mill.

One of my most memorable sawmilling experiences occurred while I was sawing down at Michael Lake. A lot of the logs we milled were cut in the Yellow Point area, which had a lot of old growth. Lloyd Gilmour, who owns the NHL Restaurant, and Frank Kilner were logging some of this timber for Miller. They brought in one twenty-foot log, about four feet or so through. Miller had taken an order for two-inch clears. We had a half-inch saw kerf, so every time you cut, you wasted a half an inch. If you cut two-inch boards, you wasted twenty percent of the wood that went down the drain in sawdust. But, that's what he wanted, so I hacked up this log and it was just a beautiful log. It cut clears right to the heart, 1,140 feet of clear, two-inch lumber out of one log. That was one of the highlights in my sawmilling career.

I did have one mishap there. One of the fellows working on the carriage was lighting a cigarette when I backed up on the carriage. He lost his balance and threw his hand out. I saw he was off balance, and realized either his hand or his whole body would go through the saws—there were two saws. I didn't hesitate on the carriage, but let it keep coming at an even speed so he could get his balance. When he threw his hand out it went through the saws and he lost three or four fingers. That was the only accident I had in twenty-seven years of sawing. I was pretty unhappy that he lost his fingers, but it was better than losing his life.

While I was sawing at that mill, some little kids used to come over and watch me work. Their father had bought a farm on Michael Lake. There were always lots of mallard ducks sitting on the lake and going into his farm, and I would sit there watching them while I worked. I went over to see him one day to ask him if I could shoot some ducks on his property and he says, "Oh, sure," so in the winter of 1946 we started shooting ducks there. I used to shoot with my brother-in-law, Nick Smith, and my old pal, Johnnie Bohoslowich. We used to have great hunting. There were lots of grouse and cock pheasants down around the edge of the fields, and we always got a variety of birds, as well as a lot of deer.

In the summer of 1946 I met a Victoria girl by the name of June Sangster. Her family had moved to Nanaimo during the war. Her father was in charge of Blue Lion Bus Transit, which was the first bus system in Nanaimo. It started with the military during the war, and after the war continued on as a civilian transportation system. Much later it was taken over as part of the present government operated transit system. It probably would have been better left as a free enterprise business.

June and I developed a relationship during the summer of 1946. I courted her right into the latter part of the year, when I thought I should get married. I asked her to marry me in November, and we got married on December 7th—Pearl Harbour Day. My mother, being Irish and very superstitious, told me, "Son, that's a bad time to be getting married. You shouldn't be getting married on a day like that."

"Well," I said. "It's the only day the Sangster family think is a good day for them."

Like Pearl Harbour, that marriage turned into a disaster. In fall of 1946, before we got married, I built a suite at 265 Pine Street in her dad, Irv Sangster's basement and that's where we lived. The following year I bought some property at 28 Wakesiah, where Jimmy Bonner lives now, and built a house.

It was very stressful building this house. I was working long hours at the sawmill, and I used to finish my dinner at night and run all the way over to the house and work on it until about 11:00 or 11:30 p.m. Then, because I didn't have a car, I'd run all the way home and catch some sleep before getting up at six in the morning and onto the job. I think I wore out about two pairs of running shoes travelling the mile between our suite and the house. I finally got that house put together with some help from Johnnie Bohoslowich and Andy Poje, and we moved into it in March of 1948.

My first daughter, Lynn, was born November 2, 1947. We lived with her for a few months in the basement suite on Pine. She used to drive me wacky. I was working hard during the days, and at night time, when I was trying to sleep, I had to keep the buggy beside me at the bed. As long as I kept rocking that buggy, she slept; as soon as I quit rocking it, she would start howling again. She had to be one of my crankiest kids, but she grew up into a jolly, happy person.

I guess maybe I started off on the wrong foot with June, because she was kind of lazy, and I was the guy who had to worry about the kids and look after them during the night. I was the guy who worked all day while she lay around doing nothing.

In the fall of 1947 I went on one of my best hunting trips since the war. The Morgan brothers from Cedar told me about the great hunting at Sayward. We went up there with an old tent to sleep in, out in the bush. The previous Christmas my mother-in-law had bought me a Timothy Eaton sleeping bag for $1.75. It was nothing to write home about, but it was the best I had at the time.

At the opening of the season we were at Sayward on a nice sunny Labour Day weekend, which was a delight to be hunting in. Quite often you didn't see much game at the beginning of the season, but the chances were always better. That night I put my sleeping bag under the car and slept there. There must have been half a dozen cars within 300 yards of where we were, and everybody was talking and carrying on, drinking beer and yapping away beside fires all night long.

The next morning it was very foggy and there was a lot of dew. I got up and had a bottle of beer for breakfast, and headed off the road, straight out into the bush. I didn't go in there very far until I came to a bit of a cedar swamp with steam coming off it. I walked out on a blown-down cedar snag and was standing there, about ten feet in the air, when out bolted a big, five-point buck from right underneath me. I could have jumped on his back. When I fired, I fell off the log and landed on my butt. I jumped up and ran after him. There was so much dew and such a lot of grass in that swamp, that it left a clear path in the grass. It was staggering back and forth badly, not leaving a straight trail. I heard a little bit of noise to my left and there was the five-pointer laying down, looking right at me, five or six feet away.

Bullets were expensive then, and I had some army bullets I'd brought home from the war; they were hard-nosed. I took the regular hunting bullet out of my rifle, and put in one of the hard nosed ones. I shot the deer right between the eyes. That deer never even blinked. It just kept on looking at me. The army issue bullet went right through his head and his brain, and out the other side and he never twitched a muscle. I cranked in a regular bullet and gave him one in the neck. That was the end of that buck. To see that bullet go through the deer's head and for it not to flinch was really strange. I know that happened to a lot of soldiers during the war. I always carried some hard-nosed bullets with me when I hunted deer, in case I saw a blue grouse, which were everywhere. When I saw a grouse I'd put one of them in and shoot its head off. Many times on hunting trips in the Sayward area—my favourite hunting area—I'd get a dozen grouse.

I hollered for the boys to come and help me with the deer. They started coming, and all of a sudden they started shooting like crazy. I heard one of them say, "We got him! We got him!" They must have fired ten shots. They had got a big black bear. One of the Morgan boy said to me, "If it wasn't for me that bear would have got away. I fired the last shot. After I fired it was just a ruined bruin, George."

"Oh, great! Now give me a hand to get this deer out of here." I gutted the deer while they were going crazy over their bear. We got the deer out and hung it up. We were smart enough to take a bit of cheesecloth with us, so we covered it up the best we could so that the blow flies wouldn't get into it. When we got back to Nanaimo we weighed that buck at Davenport Ice Cream, which belonged to Pete Maffeo at the time, and it was the biggest buck I shot in my life—210 pounds dressed.

Before we'd left camp in the morning, a European foreigner of some kind—we called them "Bohunks"—went by our camp pushing a wheelbarrow. About one o'clock that afternoon he came back, smoking his pipe and pushing his wheelbarrow with a four-pointer in it. He was a happy guy. He went down the road from us a couple of hundred yards, hung up his deer and looked after it. He also had cheesecloth to cover it up.

Later that afternoon, we all went out hunting again and the same guy comes down the road with the wheelbarrow. "What are you taking the wheelbarrow again for?" I asked him.

"Oh!" he said. "When I was down there yesterday afternoon I saw two four-pointers. I'm taking my wheelbarrow because I may get the other one this afternoon." That afternoon we got a two point and a three point, so out of the four of us we had three deer. That wasn't too bad.

We had a little fire going and we were making ourselves some supper, well after dark, when the guy comes back, smoking his pipe, with the second four-pointer in that bloody wheelbarrow. "Hey mate," I said. "Do you think that happens in this country all the time?"

"Well, I hope it does," he said. "So far it's working out quite well for me."

I didn't go hunting with the Morgan boys again, but found someone else who had wheels. The main reason I didn't go with them was because they drove too fast.

On another trip to Sayward that same year I was hunting with Johnnie, my brother Fred, and my brother-in-law, Nick Smith, who married my sister Marge. We got there late at night, pitched our tent, and went to sleep. We had drunk a lot of beer on the drive up and didn't have an alarm, so the next morning everyone slept in. I woke up first and I heard flip flap, flip flap. I looked up at the roof of the old Simpson Sears canvas tent. I could see something walking up there.

After a while I realized they were blue grouse, so I reached over and grabbed my shotgun. I just had my jockey shorts on. I opened the flap on the tent and saw that the two birds that had lit on the roof were still there. I looked down the road and there were four or five of them about thirty or forty feet away, looking at me. I let drive at them and I got three of them with the first whap. After giving them a little barrage I got six out of nine.

The boys in the tent woke up in a big hurry. "What the hell is going on?" "Hey, you guys it's broad daylight and the sun's out," I said. "We slept in. Come on get the hell out of the kip."

Three of us went off hunting, leaving Johnnie in camp. The night before, when we were pitching the tent, Fred and Johnnie had lit a great big fire, and Johnnie got it going again. We were not allowed to have a fire at that time of year. Along came the goddamned forest ranger and asked, "Who lit the fire?"

"I guess I did," Johnnie said. The forest ranger said he had to put it out. They had lit the fire against a big rotten chunk of log, and it was smouldering away. "Where am I going to get some water?" Johnnie asked.

"I've got two buckets in the back of this forestry truck," the ranger said. "You get them, go down to that river and get some water." The bank Johnnie had to go down was almost straight up and down, and it was at least 100 feet to the water. The forestry guy waited about an hour and a half while Johnnie went down and got two buckets each time to put the fire out. When the forestry fellow left, poor old John was all pooped out.

Later that year, on Armistice Day, I went hunting up at Kelsey Bay with my father, who had a car, and my brother Fred. We went to the area where I had been hunting the year before and had seen lots of deer. We went out just after daylight, shortly after it had stopped raining. My dad couldn't walk too far, so Fred and I got out and walked, between the road and the river. It was pretty steep ground and I was below some bluffs, with Fred up above.

I heard Fred fire two shots. I looked up to where they came from, and I couldn't believe my goddamn eyes. A deer came flying through the air like it was doing a high dive off a big rock bluff, about sixty feet high. Over that bluff it came and, sqeeeeeuuugh, landed within fifty feet of me. I went over looked. It was a deadly big buck. He had shot it in the heart and it bolted.

Fred was hollering and I let him yell for a while. He came to the top of the bluff and asked me, "Did you see a deer come down here?" "Oh, yeah." I says. He says to me, "What do you mean, 'Oh, yeah.'?"

"Well, here it is, right here. " I lifted the head up. He thought that was just hilarious. We had the first deer of the trip. We gutted it and got it up to the road.

My dad came along and we put it in the car, before heading out again. My dad said he would drive down the road and do some road hunting. I went down toward the river, and got up on the top of a huge stump. There used to be beautiful big trees through the Sayward Valley and the fir stumps were enormous. I climbed up on this stump, which had spring-board holes in it, to get a better view. The moment I got on top of it I heard a big commotion. At this time I wasn't using my old navy gun; I had a .30-.30 carbine I bought from Bill Cannon. Out ran a great big buck that was laying down beside the stump. It booted out of there. I took a whack at it, then a second whack. I figured I got him. It ran down an old road into the slash. The highest trees weren't ten feet high, and they were willows. Do you think I could find that deer? No way. In a panic, I ran down the road about two or three hundred yards until I hit the road I knew my father was on. He standing in front of the car with his gun leaning against the front bumper. I called him and he jumped in the car, racing up to where I was. I told him about the deer, "It's got to be in here and I'm sure I hit it. It's got to be wounded, so I'll go check the bushes and you stay right here. If it comes out, you give it a whack."

"Okay." he said, and went to get out of the car. "Where's my bloody gun?"

I guess my dad was just as panicky as the rest of the Dormans. He had the same kind of gun as I did, but his was a ranger rifle from the war years when the militia was issued .30-.30s.

"Holy Christ," he said. "I left my gun back where I was when you waved at me. " When he went back to get it, there were the tire tracks over it. After that you could not hit anything with that gun. I'm sure when he ran over it the barrel bent.

I hunted around in the bushes for a long time, but there was no way I could find that deer. It was a huge racker, and it upset me to no end, but I never found it. After that I didn't have much feeling for .30-.30s. I don't think they have enough whap to them.

I left my dad on the road and went down to the area where Fred was. I was hurrying along and got to some bushes past where Fred had been. Suddenly I saw about fifteen deer come out of the bushes, six of them bucks. They ran down toward the river, with me chasing them, into a little bit of timber along the edge of the river. Fred came along chasing the deer, too.

"Okay Fred," I told him. "You see how far that timber goes? Those bloody deer have got no place to go. It's either swim the river or bolt out of there. You go down to the other end, block the way, and come towards me. I'll wait for you here."

"Yeah, yeah," Fred said. He went down to the end of the timber, then he started coming toward me. I went into the timber and walked toward him. I heard a noise coming toward me, and hid behind a tree. A big deer came down a trail and when it was about twenty feet away I gave it a whack right in the head. Down it went, a dandy buck. My father-in-law's brother entered that deer in the Sylvester U-Drive Tournament in Victoria and it won second prize. It weighed 183 pounds.

After shooting, I stayed behind the tree and right away a couple of does followed by a three-point buck came along. I shot the buck, too.

About then I heard a whole bunch of shots from Fred. I waited a bit and then heard splashing and carrying on in the water. The rest of the deer had jumped in the river and swam across. I wasn't going to shoot one in the water, so the rest of them escaped.

"I know I got one," Fred yelled. "I wounded it! I wounded it!" We looked for it for a long time before we finally we found it, a five pointer. Now we had a four pointer, a three pointer, and two five pointers.

The next day we thought we'd go back out and hunt the same area. We were allowed two deer apiece at that time, six between the three of us. That day I ended up with two more and Fred shot one, so we had one too many. We took the back seat out of my dad's car, and stuffed in some of the deer, with the rest in the trunk, and threw the seat in on top of the deer. Fred and I squeezed into the front with my dad and we headed for Nanaimo. We never saw a game warden all the way home.

The following year, 1948, the game department decided to close down hunting in the area around Kelsey Bay where we had been. They shut it down for a couple of years. They figured the deer stock was getting depleted. When Fred and I hunted in that area we must have seen fifty deer apiece each day. Besides that, my dad saw does and fawns, as well as bucks, running across the road.

In 1950, they decided they'd open the season up again. Then we had two back-to-back winters that were the worst I think Vancouver Island saw until later in the 1960s. When we were allowed, we went back up there hunting again, but I hardly saw a deer. So much for the game department's great plan.

When we moved to Wakesiah I was still sawing for Miller. A year or so later, Miller decided he wanted to move his mill up to Williams Lake, but I didn't want to go. That winter I had no mill work, so Fred and I went falling trees in the Chase River area, on the old Canadian Collieries property, for my father-in-law. He, Ernie Graham and Ray Young had formed a company called Island Industries a few months before, and got a contract to do some logging for H. R. MacMillan Export at Nanaimo River. I had a falling contract. We felled the first trees on the other side of the bridge at Nanaimo River Camp. I'll never forget how big those trees were. We got five forty-foot logs out of those firs and still had a sixteen-inch top, which was left in the bush at that time. The fir trees were beautiful!

My falling partners were Nanaimo guys. One fellow by the name of Soup Calvery was a big guy, six-six or six-seven, with the biggest hands you ever saw. He still lives in Harewood. Another was Bill Adam, who was in the navy with me and still lives in Harewood today. I had an old IEL power saw which weighed 138 pounds, and had a five-foot bar with a handle on the end that you couldn't take off.

One of the very first trees we felled was a yellow cedar leaning on an angle. Soup and Bill put a little undercut in it, and when they made a falling cut at the back, it barber chaired. It just split up the middle like you couldn't believe. They dropped the saw and ran like hell. The tree came down, WHOP! right onto the head end of the saw and screwed it up. That was the only tree we cut down that day. We were on contract and made fifteen cents apiece.

After we got the saw fixed, we used it to fall the bigger trees. We bucked a lot of the smaller ones with a hand saw. Between us, I was the best guy on the bucking saw, so I did a lot of the bucking. Soup wasn't bad but Bill was a wipe-out when it came to using the bucking saw. I already had a lot of experience with those saws in my years of living around Five Acres and in Errington when I was a kid. It was quite easy for me to get into that business. Quite often we had trouble with the power saw jamming in the log. Fred and I used that saw the following winter, and we had the same problem. Then it had to be chopped out or cut out with a hand saw.

We were cutting this big fir one day on the side of the road. We put an undercut in it, then we cut the back cut and got our saw jammed in it. This fellow, Sheepwash, and his son came along with a Cat. He was skidding some logs down a little spur to a spar tree landing and I waved to him. He dropped his logs and came over and rammed the tree with the blade raised up as high as it would go. If that tree would have been cut off at the stump it would have fallen right back on top of that Cat, and it probably would have killed him. There were no roll bars in those days.

The saw came loose, and he put the power to it. Over went the tree. He went down, dropped off his logs, went up the road, and got some more logs. We were falling trees for the Cat to skid to the landing so they could load out while we were setting up the spar tree. He came back down the road with a turn of four or five logs, one of them a big long one. His son was walking on the side of the road beside the long log. It got jammed up against a stump, which bent it. The father wasn't paying much attention and didn't notice what was happening. The tree worked up around the stump, and just as it was getting to the end, it flipped up over the stump with a snap on it like a bull whip and hit his son right on the head. Before we could get him out of there, the boy was dead. It was sad to see this happen to the Sheepwash family.

I retired my saw at Nanaimo River Camp when George LaFluer came in from Ladysmith. He was a flamboyant guy and a hard boozer. He had the sparkiest eyes you ever saw. He was a Frenchman and was super funny. George brought in some Mercury saws. My saws weighed 138 pounds and I think his were about 90 pounds. He could take the tail end handle off his power saws and saw his way out of problems. That place was a great proving ground for power saws.

When we were falling there were more no-see-ems and mosquitoes than I'd ever seen before. Also, the bark on those trees was six inches thick if it was an inch, and there was a lot of bark dust. I never felt so itchy and bit up in my life. In those days, you did not have bug repellent. We put diesel fuel on ourselves to try and stop the bugs from biting us, but that didn't work too well.

When George got his fallers in, I scaled for three months. We paid the contractors by the thousand for falling the trees, so they had to be scaled up every day. For falling snags the fallers got twenty-four feet plus the stump diameter. Many of these stumps were five feet across, but only had three feet of good wood in the middle. The rest was all rot. I would measure the three feet then give them twenty-four feet for the snag. There were some Swedes working there who gave me a bad time about my scaling practices.

On that same show, Andy Poje was second loading on the heel boom and his brother Alex was running the 10-10 Lawrence, yarding the logs into the spar tree. We still used wooden spar trees in those days. To swing the heel boom around, there was a line from the boom that ran through a block hung off a guy line and was attached to a big chunk of log. When the loader released the brake on the Lawrence, the weight of the log would pull the heel boom around and he could get another log.

One day when I was scaling, I walked in there about 1:30 in the afternoon to say hello to Andy. I was standing there not paying attention, but he knew what was going to happen. When he let off on the brake, the log came down on my head and buckled my knees before it stopped. It should have been thirty feet in the air, but on that setting they had too long a line. It was a real shock. I was astounded that this could happen to me, and because I was not paying attention. It just goes to show that when you are in the woods, you pay attention or you could be dead. Andy and Alex knew what would happen and thought this was funnier than hell.

Any logs over forty-one feet, ten inches long couldn't go on the railway cars, because when the cars went around a corner, the logs would bind on the loads ahead and behind. One of my jobs, when my scaling was caught up, was to take a hand saw and cut the ends off the logs that were too long. All these logs were taken down and dumped at Chemainus.

When I worked at Mayo's they charged us fifty cents a day to pick us up with a bus and take us to work. At the time that was a lot of money, but we had to pay it. We had a nice bus driver by the name of Sandy McKay. He was a good man to talk with, and we had a good sized bus, so it was a pleasant journey to Mayo's in the morning.

When I went to work later out at Michael Lake, I had to pay fifty cents there too. We rode in an old Army truck with benches on either side and a canvas over the top, which hopefully didn't leak too much. We picked up more men at Yellow Point on our way to the mill. We came around a corner one day, going over a bumpy old gravel road, and the driver, Jack Miller, swerved to miss a fellow in an old pickup truck. Our truck, with eighteen guys in the back, flipped over on its side. Some of the boys got dinged up pretty good. One had a broken arm, and there were a lot of cuts and bruises.

When I worked at Wilfert's mill, an East Wellington fellow named Jack picked me up in Model A at the top of Wakesiah. I called him Hijack, because in the morning when he picked me up he said, "Hi, George," and I replied, "Hi, Jack." He charged me twenty-five cents a day for a ride. He was very reliable and a very comical man.

When I went to work for Island Industries, when Nanaimo River Camp first opened up, we had to drive up White Rapids

Road, which today is the road to Nanaimo Lakes along the Nanaimo River. We drove up there and caught a speeder on the railway tracks. That also cost us fifty cents for a ride to work.

Later, as a result of negotiations between the union and the big companies, they all had to supply buses for the men and pick them up at a lot of locations near their homes. In the last few years the big companies all stopped that. The fellows had to get to marshalling points on their own accord and there were a lot of buses for sale. I think it should have been that way in the first place. They got a ride to work every day and never paid anything for it.

While I was working at Island Industries, Frank Wilfert had a sawmill on the Nanaimo Assembly Dock. It was the same mill that I worked on years before for Surrett, before he built Eureka Sawmill. Frank cut the logs they didn't want to use at Eureka Sawmill. He hadn't been doing very well and kind of went belly up. He needed somebody to come and start that sawmill up again for him and run it. He approached me and he said he had heard a lot about me.

"Oh, great, Frank. Yeah, I'll come and work for you." Winter was coming and who wants to spend the bloody winter in the bush, wading through the snow and enduring the lay-offs?

I started the mill up with Mr. Wilfert and began sawing logs there. I was quite surprised how many good logs were sorted out at Eureka Sawmill, which cut mostly hemlock. They didn't cut cedar or fir very often. Most of the logs we got to cut were mis-sorts. This mill was a circus drive mill if I ever saw one. It was built with a haywire collection of truck rear ends, transmissions and a couple of diesel engines—671 Jimmy diesels. In the time I worked there, I learned to tear them down and put them together again, along with a fellow by the name of Hanna. I was astounded that diesel engines had so much power.

Mr. Wilfert made me boss and I was also the sawyer. He paid me good money, and I had complete control of the crew. We sawed a lot of lumber and I did real well for him.

One day in 1949 I was cutting yellow cedar. I had cut a big two-inch piece off a log and while turning the log I heard a great crash. My friend Cecil Dunn was running the edger for me at the time. Nothing was devised years ago to stop the lumber going through the edger from getting kicked back by the saws. The wood would go in crooked sometimes, and the back of the saws would fire it clean out of there like it was shot out of a cannon. In later years we installed kick-back fingers, so that when a board started to come back the fingers would still stop it. We didn't have that setup at Wilfert's.

Yellow cedar has a lot of timber bind in it, so when Cecil lifted up the rollers, the cant flew back just as it was finished. The whole thing came back. It is hard to believe that it did. There were two two-by-sixes and a two-by-three. They shot back and hit a poor guy who was standing there. He was an ex-boxer, quite an excitable fellow, but he was a real good worker and in great shape.

There was a door made of a double layer of rough one-inch lumber behind him and when those boards came back and hit him they it drove him right through the door and broke it all to hell. I heard a thump and looked up. I could see the doors were knocked out, and he was laying on the floor. I ran around to see what I could do for him. I figured the two-by-three had gone right through his guts because when I grabbed him, I got a handful of blood. I pulled him back and saw that the two-by-three had missed him. What got him were the two-by-sixes. The blood was from his hip and side.

I picked him up and packed him over to a workbench. Someone threw all the tools off, and somebody else ran and got the ambulance. Mr. Wilfert happened to be there that day. Just as he came over, the guy came to. "Jesus, Dorman, " he said. "Have you got a drink for me?" His eyes were rolling. Mr. Wilfert hollered to his son, "You go over in my drawer in the office and there's a bottle of whisky there. Go get it." We gave this fellow a few shots of whisky and got him out of there. His hip and pelvis were demolished. He was able to walk again after that, but he was never able to work again. I lost track of him after a couple of years. He was a real hard working fellow. Like I said, his career in boxing had ended and it was very unfair the way he finished up trying to make a living in the sawmill.

It was November of 1949 when I started there. The following spring, Wilfert's son Frank came to work at the mill. He had been a navigator in the air force during the war, had survived, and done quite well for himself. A few months later, his father told me Frank was going to be the boss.

Then he brought in another friend who needed a job. He was another air force type. Between the two of them, they were so hyper you would have thought they were still dodging bullets or the Luftwaffe. Those guys could not settle down. I couldn't handle them and I was thinking to myself, "Fellows, I've got to find something else."

In the summer of 1950 the Shelleys had a sawmill called Nanaimo Sawmills, next to where Nanaimo Shipyards is today, where the Moby Dick Motel is. The Shelleys were bakers from Vancouver who ran around with their silly looking 4X breadtrucks. These trucks were quite funny looking, and so was the Shelley family. The ones in Nanaimo, there were a couple of them, ran the sawmill with another relative, and none of them knew enough to pound sand in a knot hole. They approached me and I went to work for them. They gave me a much better wage than I was getting from Mr. Wilfert, and I thought, "Oh, boy! I'm getting to be known around here. Now I've had three high-priced sawing jobs which paid more than they normally paid."

I worked with them until May, 1951. There were all kinds of little things they didn't understand, which were quite easy to figure out. For instance, we had a main wood chain that kept breaking. Every time that chain broke it cost us an hour. A new chain was about $700. Although at that time our wages weren't all that much, there was no way we could fight an old worn out chain, keep fixing it, and have everybody standing around. I finally talked them into getting a new chain, but it took a lot of talking. All those guys could think about was taking money out of the company and running like hell with it. In the end the company went broke, but not while I was working there. I did enjoy working for them, and the main person I dealt with was Ken McCannell, who married into the Shelley family. He was a good man, and has passed away.

We used to cut super good logs at that mill. They brought in some nice fir logs that came off Sonora Island, from a little logging claim there. One of the logs was four and a half feet through, and twenty feet long. They were looking for all the six-by-six and wider clears we could get. This was such a good log I got a double cut of clears off it all the way around. The biggest piece I cut is one I will never forget. It was six inches by thirty-six inches of clear fir, twenty feet long. I think it went to England, where they resawed clears. That was one of the most beautiful logs I ever saw.

The superintendent was Bill Nyquist—whose daughter later married my brother Fred. He once came over to tell me how to saw the logs. "Hey, Bill, " I told him. "If you want a whole bunch of lumber down there that won't make the grade, I'll do it. You can't saw two-and-a-half by sevens out of logs with four inch knots in them. I'll get it right." Even though he was a bit of a hot head, when I said that to him he didn't get mad at me. After that he never bothered me. I went ahead and doubled production at that sawmill before I left, which was in just over a year.

I left for a good reason. About two weeks before I quit, June and I were playing bridge one night with John Fiddick and his wife Eunice, my father-in-law, Irv Sangster and his wife. I mentioned that this fellow, Swanson, who had a little mill down at Brechin Point where the BC Ferries' parking lot is today, wanted me to come and work for him. Fiddick said, "Hey, Dorman why don't you buy the bloody mill instead of working for him?"

"What with?" I asked him "Peanuts?"

"You've got your house built and you haven't got much mortgage against that. You don't owe anything but your mortgage do you? Besides, your father-in-law could give you some money. How much do you think you'd need to buy that mill?"

"I would need to have at least $20,000 in cash before we started," I told him.

"I'm sure you can get $5,000 on your house, and your father-in-law can give you $5,000. You could scrounge up the last $10,000."

"Well, I could probably try my brother and some of the Dorman relations on Bowen Island and in Vancouver."

"Good idea," he said, "Why don't you do that?"

I went and got all the Dormans riled up and managed to scrounge up the $20, 000. Then I dealt with Swanson on his mill. They were only cutting 11,500 feet a day at that time. He had some inventory, and I ended up paying him $44,000 for the inventory and the sawmill. He had some good lumber contracts to cut, old war-time contracts. He wanted to know how I was going to pay for it. I said, "I'll pay $2.50 a thousand board feet." To him, that didn't seem like much money because he was only cutting 11,500 a day average. I took that mill over and within three and a half months had it cutting 35,000 feet per shift. By 1954 I had it cutting 35,000 a shift, double shift. That was my beginning in the sawmill business.

George Dorman
leading the
Nanaimo pipe
band, in Nanaimo.

George Dorman
(l) and Jim
Donaldson in
Nanaimo Pipe
Band uniforms
in front of
George's house
on Wakesiah in
1953.

George Dorman
on his second
honeymoon on
the Oregon
coast, with a
redwood log,
1954.

George Dorman
with a pile of elk
and deer horns, at
Yellowstone Park
in 1954.

George Dorman on head saw at G.W.Dorman Pulp Chip Co. in 1961. "I always stood when I sawed."

Johnnie
Bohoslowich
with Canada
geese in Alberta,
1961.

G.W. Dorman Pulp & Chip had a log dump at Union Bay, where logs would be boomed or loaded onto trucks to go to Nanaimo.

Harold "Bookie" Mayovsky (l) worked for G.W. Dorman Pulp & Chip as bookkeeper, foreman and manager from 1959 to 1984. He was one of the first graduates of Malaspina College and died in 1992 at age 51. Terry Rodway (r) worked for the company for 14 years and died in 1992. Photo taken in East Kootenays in 1963, returning from hunting trip to Alberta.

Brian, Kevin and George Dorman at their Long Lake house, with salmon caught at Rivers Inlet, 1967.

Art Morgan's convertible after he felled a tree on it on Hammond Bay Road.

George Dorman with gommier logs cut for a test run, at Roseau, Dominica, 1967. The logs were shipped to New York and trucked to West Virginia where they were cut.

Planks cut on a test run of gommier logs in West Virginia.

Nanaimo Daily Free Press

Nanaimo Logger Aids Dominican Economy

Two Nanaimo men, George Dorman and Bob Malpass, have taken Canadian forest products know-how technique and capital to a tiny Caribbean island in a major effort to strengthen the economy of the Leeward Islands.

Together with Ted Osborne and Jack Wilson of Vancouver, and with the financial involvement of the Canadian government, they have formed Dom-Can Timbers Ltd., a $1,500,000 logging and sawmilling enterprise on the island of Dominica, a possession of the United Kingdom and a point selected for development by Ottawa.

LEAVES FOR ISLAND

Mr. Dorman, who returned to Nanaimo in the fall after conducting initial field work in Dominica, leaves with his wife and children to take up a 18-month residence on the Island in two weeks' time.

"Bob Malpass will be looking after the logging end of things down there," said Mr. Dorman today, "and I shall be building the mill and getting it into operation."

Mr. Dorman said Ottawa had indicated to one of the Vancouver partners in the enterprise its interest in the development of Dominica and willingness to provide investment capital for use there.

Investigation disclosed excellent economic possibilities and the development company was formed.

Involved is construction of a sawmill with a 25,000,000-foot per year capacity, the product of which in the main will find market in the Leeward Islands.

Top grade lumber will find market in the United States, where it will be consumed in furniture manufacturing.

Mr. Dorman said today the

GEORGE DORMAN

chief species to be processed by the company is known as gommier, a type of mahogany but stronger and of denser grain than mahogany itself.

"There are other species," he said, "and they are in the main hardwoods."

"They really don't resemble anything we have on Vancouver Island."

Mr. Dorman said he expects to have the mill in operation by April.

All told, the project will provide employment for about 70 Dominicans initially, after a two-year training period.

Start-up will be directed by experienced Canadians, but the semi - independent Government of Dominica requires their departure after two years and in turning over of the operation, if possible, to Dominicans at that time.

Construction of the modern mill, the first-ever in Dominica, began in November, and the project is about half-finished.

The company has been awarded a 25-year lease by the gov-

ernment of Dominica authorizing the cutting of 1.3 billion feet.

The company will be taxed on a stumpage arrangement.

"I don't want to say what the stumpage will be," said Mr. Dorman.

"But it is a heck of a lot less than we pay here, I can tell you that."

The company has been given an exclusive franchise, providing that no other logging and milling enterprises may be established in the Leeward Island for 15 years.

The Island of Dominica has a population of about 70,000, virtually entirely negroid, and encompasses only 300 square miles.

It is a tiny dot on the atlas, some 800 miles south of the Dominican Republic (with which, incidentally, it is not to be confused: it is a U.K. possession).

Temperatures run in the high 80s year around and the island is about 150 miles clear of the hurricane zone.

"We are looking forward very much to getting this thing off the ground," said Mr. Dorman.

"All of us see in it a wonderful opportunity for economic development of the Leewards, and investment prospects are excellent, too."

Mr. Dorman's interests in Nanaimo, the G. W. Dorman Pulp Chip Co. Ltd. with premises on Stewart Ave., will be administered by present senior staff members in his absence in Dominica.

Mr. Dorman said logging and milling were unknown in Dominica prior to the advent of Dom-Can Timbers Ltd., and a major training program would be involved if native personnel were to assume operation of the woods and plant projects in two years' time.

Edward Shillington (l), owner of the Dominica sawmill site, with Shirley Dorman, George Dorman and Edress Shillington.

Dominican women packing bananas on their heads to lighters loading a ship anchored offshore, 1968.

Unloading sawmill equipment from landing barge in Dominica.

Second landing barge ready to unload in Dominica.

Office built by George Dorman at mill in Dominica.

George Dorman steering carriage onto track during construction of sawmill in Dominica.

The plantation house where the Dormans lived in Dominica.

Bob Malpass with Pat Carney in Dominica, 1968

The Dominica sawmill at completion in 1968.

Logs cut in Dominica for U.S. Plywood.

5

THERE HAD BEEN OTHER SAWMILLS at Brechin Point previous to the Swanson mill we took over. Beban had the first mill there. At that time the water came up to the traffic lights at the entrance to the ferry terminal. The area that is now parking lot was filled in with sawdust, slabs, log ends, and rubbish. When they built the parking area they just dumped rocks off the far end of the lot. If they wonder why it keeps settling, it's because of what was used to fill in that area. I think Beban was the instigator, followed by Swanson and then Dorman.

The mill, which we renamed Brechin Lumber, needed a lot of work on it before we started cutting up logs. My old friend Johnnie Bohoslowich decided he would come to work for his old pal and be a millwright. He was working as a carpenter for a fellow by the name of Quantz, who had his own little business building houses, doing renovations, and so on. Johnnie told Quantz he wanted to quit, but that he would like to try the millwright job first.

Johnnie came down and worked a week for me in the sawmill. It was so haywire. Every time you turned around we found something broken. But Johnnie didn't like all that sawdust down his neck and the problems that go along with being a millwright. So, at the end of the week he said, "I think I'll go back hammering nails Monday morning." Working at the mill, he sweated like crazy. I think Johnnie had a nervous streak after his six and a half years in the Royal Navy. He went through hell in the Navy. I think he was nervous, scared something was going to go wrong. If you don't know what you are doing around machinery, you get nervous. It just wasn't his bag, so he went back to carpentering. I kind of laughed. I missed my one-week millwright pal.

The first change I made was to lengthen the carriage so that I could cut forty-foot logs. The original carriage was twenty feet, so I extended it to thirty feet, and put an air set and works onto the carriage. That gave us a better set, but we still didn't have very good log-turning facilities. We used the canting gear or turned the logs by hand, which was easy for me because I had been doing it for Miller for thirty-four months, and at Mayo's before that.

The edger was no good, so I put in a ten-inch edger I got from Hillcrest Lumber. It worked very well for us. It would handle anything up to ten inches thick, and went down to three inches. All the lumber was hand trimmed. There was no barker or burner. We had a big slashing saw and threw all the slabs and waste into the slasher, which cut it into firewood lengths that went up into a bunker. A truck could pull in underneath and take away the firewood, which we sold around Nanaimo.

Once I got the mill operating, I got production up with a lot of super hard work. I created a lot of bad feelings with a few people. When we took that mill over, there were so many dogs working there that Swanson had never got around to getting rid of. I fired guys right and left until I got a proper crew.

My brother Fred was a partner. On weekends he was busy with his father-in-law building houses but I was usually in there working. My responsibility was to saw the logs and Fred ran the outside end, looking after the planer and seeing that the lumber got shipped out.

When we began, there was a fellow by the name of Johns, who was in the firewood business, who took away our waste wood. After a while I decided I was going to get a wood truck; why let someone else make money off it. I bought a wood truck for $750, which put Fred's nose out of joint. He figured he should own half of it.

"Fred," I said. "You're giving me a pain in the ass. I'll give this truck to Reg if he wants it." Reg was working for Mayo's at the time, driving a flat deck hauling lumber out of McKay Lake. I phoned him up and said, "Eh, you want to get into our wood business and have a truck? I bought a truck. You can pay me back for it as you can."

Reg came down and had a look around. He quit Mayo's and took over the wood business at Brechin Lumber. That's where Reg Dorman got his start in the trucking business. Over the years he had as many as forty-five trucks. Today he's back to one, which he drives himself. That's the way things go in Nanaimo. There are so many trucks around Nanaimo now that if you own a truck you've got to drive it yourself; you can't afford to pay a driver.

We had a fellow working in the office who was an old Canadian Collieries man by the name of Walter Caverly. When Fred and I were kids we sold him four or five cords of alder firewood every year. My father helped build a house for him behind Harewood School with the help of us kids.

We filled some interesting orders at Brechin Lumber. Foss Launch and Tug from Seattle had all kinds of wooden tugs, and barges. We sold them a million feet or so of yellow cedar every year. I got most of my yellow cedar logs from my friend, Bob Malpass, which he logged off of Wolf Mountain. I also got some from Teddy Osbourne at Sechelt.

Foss was building a new tug and needed two pieces of clear yellow cedar for keel timbers on two tugs they were building. They wanted two ten-by-twenties, free of heart centre, forty-one feet long. "Oh, boy!" I thought. "I know where the log is to cut them from." I had been up in the bush with Bob and saw a deadly yellow cedar standing there. I asked him if that tree was still there? It was. I went out in the bush and sized up the tree. There wasn't a knot for about forty-six feet.

Walker Addison and his brother, George, felled it. The Addison's were old-time fallers in Nanaimo, working at Northwest Bay for MacMillan Bloedel and others. They cut it down and I looked at the butt. There wasn't a blemish in that butt, which had to be about forty inches in diameter. We cut that lovely yellow cedar off at forty-three feet. There wasn't a knot in it and there wasn't a mark in the top.

I took it down to the sawmill and cut two ten-by-twenties out of it, leaving four inches in the centre. There was not a knot in either one of those pieces. Today if you had the same logs you'd be rich. There are still a lot around in the mountains, but all the big guys have them. Something like that today would be worth way up in the tens of thousands of dollars.

Foss continued to buy from me until they went out of wooden boats about 1958, when they started building steel boats. Instead of buying a million or more feet of yellow cedar once a year from me, they dropped down to two or three hundred thousand, and finally the thing fizzled out in the early 1960s.

I was working real hard getting that mill going, and was at my prime. We turned logs by hand and I used to be able to snap off peavey handles a foot down from the top. We had a lot of trouble with the roller behind the head rig. I sent Fred Barr, our millwright, up to Gorosh's to see if he could find a stronger roller to put in its place. Fred got a roller that was solid steel, eight or nine inches through. Gorosh sold things by the pound, and he weighed it at 370 pounds.

Fred got back to the mill at lunch hour and had it in the back of a truck. He was going to get the guys to give him a hand to take it into the millwright's room. We were going to mount some bearings on it and get it ready to put in behind the head saw.

"Oh, I can pack that," I said.

"No you won't," he said, "It weighs 370 pounds."

"Well, let's see if I can or not." We had a bit of a ramp that went up about three feet and was about twelve feet long. I lifted it up in my two arms out of the truck and said, "Yeah, I can carry that." I packed it up the ramp right in front of all the employees and plunked it onto the bench.

I used to be super strong. Once, when I was working at Michael Lake we had a twelve-by-twelve, twenty feet long, to load in a truck. Myself and another muscular young fellow lifted it up to slide it into the truck. I picked up my end quite easy and the other guy was having a bit of trouble. I said to him, "Hey, I bet you I can pick up this by myself."

"You've got to be kidding," he said.

"I bet I can." I took hold of the middle of that twelve-by-twelve, got it balanced just right and I lifted it off the ground. We figured it weighed close to 400 pounds. It's no wonder in my bar room brawling days I used to pick up all the guys and either squash 'em or huck 'em. Not that many people ever picked up that kind of weight in their lifetime. Just being a working fellow, I got real strong. That's what I was—a *worker*.

While I was getting the mill off the ground, my wife June was quite sick. She had a hysterectomy and after that she was out of control. In 1952 I caught her in bed with one of my good pals in the Ritz Hotel in Vancouver. Another time I caught her acting up on her back in my friend's car. Then she ran off with one of my friends in May, 1953. At the time I was very upset about it. I forgave her the first two times, but I sure as Christ didn't the third time. I was left with two young girls to raise.

The day she left, I was working down at my sawmill. I came home, had my lunch and a quick little love in. I didn't have much time. I had to get going. I went back to work, and when I came home about 5:30 that night, she wasn't there. I heard the kids crying; they were locked in their bedroom. I was really brassed off. I didn't know where she had gone. There was no note or explanation of what she was doing. Two weeks later, I tracked her down in Vancouver. I had a talk with her and immediately divorced her.

Later that year, in the summer of 1953, I was driving along Stewart Avenue in an old beat up truck I had inherited when I bought the mill from Swanson. I saw a girl I'd known from years before. We'd once had a sex relationship and I hadn't seen her since the end of the war. She was moving into a house, so I stopped and waited while she talked to the movers, who were going somewhere to pick up some more of her stuff.

"Come on in and see my house," she said.

We went in and right away I started thinking about having some sex. "Those movers are going to be back in a minute," she said. "How are we going to have sex when I have to watch for those guys."

"Get up on your hands and knees on the chesterfield and watch for them out the window," I suggested. I snuggled in behind her and had a nice little time.

When we were done she said, "I guess you're finished. Do you want me to run downstairs now and bark at the cars as they drive by?"

That same year I went to the Truck Loggers' convention in Vancouver. One of the women there that I knew quite well— she was married—was always kidding me about sex. We were at a party one night that was going to go on for a while and she said, "Come on over to my room and I'll see if you're any good at sex."

We went over to her room, leaving her husband, who was all pissed up, at the party. It was the same old story, a stiff cock has no conscience. We had a rattle and were lying there naked having a drink when there was a rap at the door.

"I know that rap," she said. "It's got to be my husband."

"What the fuck am I going to do?"

"Hide under the bed," she said. "He's all drunk. I'll just give him a blow job and when he starts snoring you can get out from under the bed and get the hell out of here."

About twenty minutes later he started snoring and I crawled out. She saw me to the door and I was laughing so goddamn hard I just about pissed on the floor. He just kept on snoring, so I thought, that's fair enough.

That same summer I met up with a woman who had just broken up with her husband. He was in Vancouver. We'd had sex at her house and were drinking a beer, thinking about a second time, when a whole bunch of hollering started downstairs. I jumped up, grabbed my clothes and hid in the closet.

She went downstairs to talk to her husband. They were yelling at each other and I thought I'd better get out of there. I climbed out the window and was hanging onto the gutter, trying to edge around to a carport on the side of the house, about thirty feet off the ground. As I got to the corner the bloody gutter started to give out and I just managed to edge onto the roof. I chinned myself over the side of the carport onto the ground and ran like hell to my truck, laughing like hell. It wouldn't have been so funny if that gutter had let go and I'd fallen three stories.

Just after June cleared out on me in May, I met a German girl through Ron MacIsaac, whose name was Anita Barzak. I went out with her for a while and at first she was very nice. But she got a little too pushy with me eventually, so I ended that. While I was involved with her, her father talked me into taking him hunting. He was one of these arrogant Germans who claimed he fought in Russia.

In the fall of '53 we went off deer hunting at the beginning of the season. I took my brother-in-law Nick, my brother Fred, Johnnie, Jake Fhee and Barzak. That night, when we got on the road up to our favourite hunting spot, we found that a big, old railway trestle we used had been condemned, so there was no way to drive across the river into where we wanted to camp. We decided to take our sleeping bags and walk in. I still had that Timothy Eaton sleeping bag; one good thing about it was that it was plenty light, so it was easy to carry. We had a few beers, gathered up a bit of food, and away we went.

It was about 9:30 when we started and by 10:30 the others wanted to know how far we were going to go. Johnnie had started calling the German fellow Flour Sacks, and soon everyone else was too. Johnnie didn't much like Germans at this time, after spending six years fighting them in the Royal Navy and losing his brother to boot.

We were getting up the mountain and about 11:00 I said "Just a little further." Flour Sacks was getting tired. Everyone else was laughing. Jake Fhee must have been carrying about six bottles of beer that he was drinking. Finally, at about 11:45, we decided we had gone far enough. We thought we'd get some sleep and be up at daylight. We figured we were way ahead of the other guys coming behind us, and they would chase all the deer our way. We laid down on the ground and got as comfortable as we could with our sleeping bags.

There were quite a few bears around that area at the time and Jake paced up and down most of the night. "There's bears here. I hear them, there making noises in the bush," he complained.

"For Christ sake," I told him. "Lay down and go to sleep."

He was a fat turkey, but a good pal, younger than Johnnie and
I.

The next morning when we went hunting, Jake and I
started up the road with Johnnie. The other three went off on a
road to the right and hunted around the bottom of a little
mountain that had a bunch of timber on it. They saw a lot of
deer but no bucks.

Jake and I got quite a bit ahead of Johnnie and after a while
we heard a lot of shooting behind us, twelve shots in all. We
didn't know what was going on; and didn't think Johnnie
would be firing that many shots. When we headed down the
road we could see, away down on the flat, a guy waving
something above an object lying on the ground. We thought
somebody might have got shot, so we ran down the road for all
we were worth.

When we got closer we saw it was Johnnie with a huckle-
berry bush, waving it over this one-horned, five-point buck
lying on the road.

"What the hell are you doing," I asked him. "What's the
story?"

"I'm keeping the blow flies off my deer. For Christ sake,
give me a hand." Poor Johnnie, he was sweating hard and the
other guys were nowhere in sight.

"We heard twelve shots; what was that?"

"Yeah, goddamn deer," he said. "I was a little slow and
you guys ran off and left me. Those other clowns chased this
deer and it ran across the road between me and you guys. I
started shooting at it. First shot, I missed. The deer just stood
and looked at me. The next shot, I blew one of its horns off. It
started running around in circles. I kept shooting at it and got
buck fever so bad I kept missing. But I got him on the twelfth
shot. I ran out of soft nose after shot number nine and used some
of those army bullets you gave me." That was probably the
biggest deer Johnnie ever got.

On another occasion I was hunting with my friends Walter
Cooper, Ekey Baird and Larry Rafter—Pop-gut Rafter, my boys
used to call him. We had gone up to Sayward and pitched the
leaky old Simpson Sears tent.

In the morning it was raining and Rafter wouldn't get out of the kip, so three of us went up the mountain hunting. We were gone most of the day and by three in the afternoon had got a scrubby little two-point. The rain was coming down hard and when we came back to the tent we came in from the other direction, behind the tent.

Pop-gut Rafter was in the tent, which faced up the road. The first thing we wanted was a beer. Our tongues were hanging out. We were soaking wet and so was everything else. That tent leaked like a sieve.

"Hey, do me a favour you guys. How about walking up the road and gutting that deer for me. You're already wet." I looked up the road and about forty yards from the tent there was a deer. That guy was laying in his sleeping bag at about ten in the morning, drinking beer, and the deer came walking down the road. Pop-gut waited until it got close to the tent and shot it. He wouldn't even get out of the tent to gut it. Ekey and I went and gutted it out, a little two point. Rafter was always doing things the easy way. But if there were ten beers and four guys, he could drink six of them.

I met my second wife that summer. I had seen her down at Michael Lake when the little kids used to come and watch me all the time. In the late 1940s and early 1950s, when Johnnie Bohoslowich, Andy Poje and I used to hunt on the Judson farm, she was a little girl with her finger in her mouth. She worked in the barn milking cows in the morning or shovelling dung. "Hey, you guys," I told Johnnie and Andy. "One day I might come back here. That's the kind of a girl I would like to marry." They all laughed like hell.

Her father used to bring logs into my sawmill. One day I asked him, "Would you mind, Fred, if I were to marry your daughter, Shirley?"

"I don't think she can do any worse," was his only answer. Well, thanks a lot, Fred.

Well, lo and behold, I started courting her and we got married on Friday the 13th of August, 1954. My mother warned me again, "Friday the 13th is a bad day," just like she warned me about my first marriage on Pearl Harbour Day. "George, you shouldn't get married on a bad day. It's bad luck, Friday the 13th."

That summer, just before we got married I needed to have another haemorrhoids operation. I was hunting with my friend Johnnie and Jack Stewart up in Sayward. We had shot a couple of deer and on the Sunday morning I chased a deer into the river. I shot it in the river and went in to get it. I almost drowned over that deer. It got away on me in the heavy current. I was lucky I didn't get sucked down the river, because it went into a real bad canyon.

After that, I was bleeding quite bad from my rectum. I said to the others, "Hey, you guys we got to get out of here. I just can't handle this pain any longer." When we drove home I was in bad pain. We were using my friend, Jack's truck.

It was late Sunday afternoon when we arrived home. I phoned up the doctor and told him how bad I was feeling. He said to me, "You get up here first thing in the morning and I'll examine you." I went in the next morning for my examination, and I was bleeding badly. The doctor lined me up with Dr. Whaley in Vancouver, in a medical building right across the street from the Vancouver Hotel.

Shirley came along to drive my big Chrysler I'd just bought, a two door. We were driving down Pine Street in Nanaimo, and she was in a hurry to get me to the ferry. Somebody came up a side street and ran into us.

A friend of mine by the name of Ken Wright, an old air force man who still lives in Cedar today, lived on that corner. He saw what happened and when I told him I had to catch a ferry, he gave me a ride while Shirley stayed behind to straighten up the mess with the car.

Off to Vancouver I went. Dr. Whaley was a great specialist with haemorrhoids operations and it went as smooth as can be, with none of the pain I had in 1946. I understand now that haemorrhoids operations aren't much problem at all, but the first one was a very tough one.

Not long after Shirley and I got married I got into some real good sawmilling. Victoria had started logging in the watershed and they had a whole bunch of logs all piled up. We had a look at them and put a bid. I was the successful bidder and had a hard time scrounging up the money to pay for them, but I managed to get it.

A trucker by the name of Patterson from Duncan hauled the logs from the Victoria watershed down to Mill Bay. We dumped them in the water, sorted them, boomed them up, and brought them to Nanaimo. There were 4.5 million feet of logs out in front of our mill, which even today is a lot of logs. They were the greatest logs I ever cut in the Brechin Lumber mill. We cut them into all kinds of timbers and interesting lumber for Australia and other places.

One of the boys working on the carriage wanted to use my truck to go home for lunch one day. "Okay Bill," I said. "But the truck needs gas, so fill it up at the pumps. The pump on the right, when you are facing them, is diesel, and the pump on the left is gas. Don't screw up."

He buggered off and by the time the rest of us finished lunch, he wasn't back. I found somebody else while we were waiting and we carried on without him. He came back about half an hour later. "What the hell happened to you?" I asked.

"Oh, there's something wrong with your truck. It keeps smoking, and carrying on, and doesn't want to keep running."

"Look, you silly bastard," I said. "Which pump did you use?"

"You told me to use the one on the right."

"No, I didn't. I said the one on the right has the diesel in it, use the one on the left which has gas in it. You've got diesel in that truck and that is why it won't go. You've got a new name. You're the 'Diesel Engineer', Bill. Now get on the carriage and let's get going." I got somebody to drain the diesel out of the truck and get it running. It was working by the time I had to go home. That was the kind of life we had around there.

I had a fellow driving our carrier for a while. We moved the lumber around with a carrier, a four wheel machine which straddled the lumber and picked up the load to move it wherever we needed it. When I first took over the sawmill this fellow's two brothers and his father worked there too. They were part native and were good workers, as long as long as I could keep them working. But as soon as they got their pay cheques I could forget about seeing them for two or three days. I finally got rid of the father. He was the worst.

They used to live right across the road from where I later built the chip plant. Their mother, who died two or three years ago, worked on the booms when the old man boomed logs back in the 1930s and '40s for Howie Ormand. Her husband had the job but he would never go to work, so she'd go boom up the logs. They used to call her the "Boom Cat." After I got rid of the old man, the three boys worked for me on and off until the late 1960s.

In the 1950s it seemed we had a lot of shutdowns in the woods for fire season, and when that happened some of my logger friends, such as Andy Poje, would come to work at the sawmill. Andy liked to work on the boom; he was born with caulk boots on his feet. When working on the boom for me he fell in the water nearly every day, so I named him the "Daily Dipper." It was always a howl. You would look down and there he would be—in the water. Pud Ward, who also spent some time booming for me, wasn't as bad, but he was in the water a few times, too. Myself, I might have had the odd swim.

There was another funny incident at Brechin Lumber towards the end of the '50s. We used to have a few beers in the office after work every night. One Friday night a guy arrived at the office when we were drinking our beer. He had twelve boom chains and wanted to sell them. I went out and looked at them, and they were good boom chains. I knew, sure as hell, he had stolen them, but that didn't bother me. He wanted $5.00 each for them, so I gave him sixty dollars and away he went.

When I bought the chains I noticed a couple of tags on them. The next Tuesday night we were having our beer again, and here came the same guy. "I've got twelve more chains.", he said, "Do you want to buy them?"

"Let's have a look at them," I said.

He had a pickup truck, so I went out and looked in the back of the truck. I spotted the two tags right away. "Yeah, Okay. You take them out and throw them on the ground here."

"Same deal?" he asked.

"Same deal." I went back in the office and carried on

drinking beer with the boys. He put the chains down and came in. "Are you going to give me the sixty dollars?"

"You know what I'm going to give you," I answered. "Two black eyes, Mate. I recognize those chains." I walked out the door to where he had dropped the chains. "You see those two tags? That's where you put the chains Friday night. You're putting them in the same place, and they're the same chains. Don't tell me different because I recognize them. If you don't want me to punch you up, you'd better get in that pickup and get out of my sight."

One day when Andy Poje wasn't working in the bush and was down at my mill having his daily dip, he didn't have a ride home. I told him to hang on and I would give him a ride. We decided to go to the Newcastle and have a couple of beers. We were driving along Stewart Avenue in this old beat up Chev truck I inherited from Swanson, and at the end of Townsite Road a guy came along in an old truck. It was an old Model A-type truck with pieces of canvas hanging off the sides of it, and he pulled out in front of me.

"Watch this, Poje," I said. I didn't even try to miss him. I hit him right in the back end. Over went his truck, and skidded along on its side. We stopped and I had a bit of a bent wheel. The guy got out of his truck and we went over to have a look. He must have had about 200 dozen eggs in the back of that truck. He had a bunch of shelves built in, with eggs stacked on them. When the truck got knocked over and fell on its side the eggs were scrambled all over the road.

"You goddamned egg rancher," I said to him. "Why didn't you watch what you were doing? There was a stop sign there."

"I didn't see you."

"I didn't see you either, buddy. See you." We left him there, swearing and cursing at me. "Smarten up, egg rancher," I said, and drove away. I never heard another word about it, but anyhow, it was good for a laugh.

While I was running Brechin Lumber, a lot of jobs came up for bids to cut lumber for the Nanaimo schools, and we were quite successful in getting them. Something they always needed were two-by-fourteens, twenty-six and twenty-eight feet long. They were used for ceiling joists in most of the schools. It was interesting cutting them. You had to have good logs. We would cut a full two-inch plank, and run them through the planer and edge them to thirteen and a half inches wide, but leave them a full two inches in thickness.

I can look at houses all over Nanaimo, go in the basements and look up at the joists, and know those are my joists because there was nobody else who ever cut that size of lumber in Nanaimo. Today when you buy a joist it is only one and a half inches thick, but we used to give them a full two inches. That was a real bargain.

One of the things we did a lot of at Brechin Lumber, which we knew was illegal but which nobody seemed to enforce, was to buy beachcomb logs off anybody who had any to sell. We paid for them by cheque and had a record of it all, of course. One day the Forest Service decided to check up on us and found out we'd cut almost three million feet of beachcombed logs without going through the proper authorities. They fined us something like $250, which wasn't all that bad. But then we had to pay something like $4.00 or $5.00 a thousand in stumpage. That hurt, but it was one of the things that made the sawmilling business exciting in those days.

When I took over the mill from Swanson, I got with it some orders from MacMillan and Bloedel. They were left-over war orders for England. There was a schedule that came out every so often, and some of them were in the $80-a-thousand range, with others going up to $110 and $120 a thousand.

I started by cutting up all the low price orders first, before moving on to the higher priced ones. When I began cutting the $110 wood, M&B phoned up and took the orders off me. They finished up cutting them at their Chemainus mill.

The fellow that phoned me about that was a great British Columbia champion basketball player by the name of Chapman, who was working for M&B. He and I had a big argument about it. I was quite vexed with the rotten bastard for taking the orders off me. It was only a short time later that he had a heart attack and died. That made me think there was some kind of justice in the world.

After we stopped cutting for M&B I got hooked up with Al MacMillan and Don King, who later formed Compac Timber. Previous to that they both were working for the East Asiatic Company and at that time Al used to call on me. One time I managed to sell him some fir for Australia. The Australians called Douglas fir "Oregon fir." I sold them 500,000 feet of six-by-six and wider, up to twelve-inch. Most of the six-by-sixes I cut had a heart center in them. The lumber was all cut up and on the dock, but in the meantime, the market fell in Australia. By the time they shipped that lumber it had sat around on the docks in Nanaimo all summer in the hot sun. The heart centers shrank and cracked so badly I could stick my finger in them. When this lumber got to Australia, the Australians cried bloody hell. I don't know what happened to East Asiatic but I'm sure they had a claim against the lumber. I never had any trouble. I got my money and ran like hell, which is always the best idea if you have anything to do with lumber or logs.

After Al and Don formed Compac Timber, we became good pals and did a lot of business, mainly in the UK. Later, in 1966, they got together with Herb Doman and the East Asiatic Company to form Eacom Timber Sales, which is still operating. Don still runs Compac Timber on a part-time basis, and Al died of cancer in the late 1980s.

As I had noticed when she was a kid shovelling shit out of her old man's barn, Shirley was a real hard worker. After we were married she took on the job of raising my two daughters. On June 29, 1955, my son Brian was born in the old Nanaimo Hospital. I went up there to see him born. For women who have babies, I might say, that's no easy chore. I'll never forget that. I always have a great feeling for mothers because they go through a lot to be pregnant and have a child, let alone raising them later.

As I mentioned earlier, the geniuses in the game department shut down hunting around Kelsey Bay for almost three years, and then opened it up to shooting does. Great! A highly intelligent bunch of school boys going to university in Vancouver are put in charge of our game department. All we've ever had was school boys. They go and get a little idea in the university, and get a little badge "I'm a Game Warden" or, "I took this up and I know what I am talking about." Well, there are many old guys like myself who have hunted in the bush for years and years, and know as well as anybody else that if you kill off the breeding stock, you are not going to build up the herd. For instance, you don't see the farmer shooting his cows and bulls if he wants to build up a herd. He might shoot the bull and get another one, but you don't shoot the cows too.

The year they reopened hunting, I was in the Camp Five area, back of Menzies Bay, with Fred, Nick and Johnnie. I dropped them off and went road hunting. I came to a big burn and there was a huge buck standing out there. It had rained like hell that morning and the sun had just come out. It was a fresh burn, black and shiny. The buck was standing way out there with the sun shining on him, just like in a picture. I don't think many people have seen that, where the ground is black as can be and there's a big buck standing there. I had my old army gun with me, so I took aim and thought, "Dorman, you ought to aim a little high." I went whap and down went the buck. I got out of my car and thought, "Hmm, he's not going anywhere," so I opened a bottle of beer. As I was drinking my beer, I heard a truck coming. Up drove a couple of boys, about twenty years old, drinking beer. "Hey, fellas," I said. "How are you doing?"

They said, "Great!"

"I shot a deer way out there. How about doing me a favour and give me a hand to drag it out."

"Oh, we'll go and get it for you." they said. These guys were eager beavers and I thought, "Oh boy, I'm sucking these boys in." I pointed out where the deer was. When they saw it they went and got it. By the time they got back I had the table set—that is, I had a couple of beers on the hood for them. They brought the deer over, gave me a hand to gut it, and throw it in the truck. And, ha, ha, ha, down the road I went. That became one of my favourite expressions, meaning: I've got something. I've lucked out. Ha, ha, ha. Down the road I went.

I found my pals and we hunted for the rest of that weekend. We were staying in my leaky old Simpson Sears tent. We did get two more deer before the end of that hunting trip, which wasn't very good for us in those years. We usually always managed to get more than that. That was in the latter part of October.

The same group of us came back later that year, which happened to be on the opening of doe season. We weren't interested in shooting does, which we don't do to this day. We drove in on an old logging railroad grade and put up the Simpson Sears tent again. It was raining like there was no tomorrow.

When we got up in the morning we went down an old railroad grade to hunt. The four of us were walking along and four deer ran across in front of us. One of them was a four-pointer. It was up all guns and pow! pow! pow! pow! Down went the buck. Johnnie was on my right and he started yelling, "I got him! I got him!" He was really excited, thinking he'd got a deer.

He was running down the track ahead of the rest of us, shouting "I got him! I got him!" The deer was in the ditch, deader than hell. I was quite surprised; I thought it would still be alive. We gutted it and dragged it in the bush to hide it. I said to Johnnie when we were standing there, "How do you figure you got him?"

"I know when I fired, that deer dropped." he said.

"Johnnie," I said. "You were on my right. I didn't hear that gun go off."

"You've got to be kidding," he said. He was really surprised.

"Let me look at that bloody gun." I took the gun off him. It was my gun and I knew he had only five bullets in it. There were still five bullets in that goddamned gun. He hadn't even fired. He was so excited, he thought he'd got it.

That was the beginning of a hilarious day. We carried on, with Fred and Nick heading off up a spur to the left, and Johnnie and I going straight ahead. It had just stopping raining and up above us the sun had started to break through a bit and was shining on the top of a bluff.

Johnnie and I were going around a bend when a shot rang

out and a big ripper tore up the ground about four inches from my foot. I was wearing an old bone dry coat and a bone dry hat, so I was sort of the colour of a deer. That ripper ricocheted off the bank to the right of me, splintered up, and went behind Johnnie. I looked up the hill and hollered like hell. There was some bloody guy up there. He looked like an older man, tall and skinny looking, all bent over.

"Give him the works," I said to Johnnie. "But don't kill the bastard—miss him. You shoot to the right, I'll shoot to the left." Johnnie gave him five to the right and I gave him five to the left. I bet that son of a bitch is still running in his grave, because we sure scared the shit out of him. I doubt if he ever shot at an another guy. That's what happens when you have doe season. Every idiot in the country comes out and shoots at everything that moves. After that incident, Johnnie was gun shy. I guess he hardly ever went in the bush hunting after that.

He was also worried about getting lost. He usually managed to get lost when I left him alone. One of the few times we went out together again, we were hunting on nice flat ground by the Salmon River where there was a lot of big timber. It was impossible to get lost there. I sent Johnnie off by himself and was walking along, admiring the trees and hoping to find a buck.

I heard a noise behind me and turned around, but I didn't see anything. Several times I heard noises and kept turning around, and I never ever saw anything. One time I turned around before I heard a noise, and who the hell is behind me but my pal Johnnie. He was sneaking from tree to tree behind me because he was scared he was going to get lost.

I called him over and said, "Come on, John, for Christ sake, come with me, you silly bastard. How the hell can you get lost around here, down on the flats?"

"Ever since that guy shot at us, I'm scared. I want to stay by you." he said. That day we saw one buck across the river. When I went to shoot at it, it bolted and got away.

When we were walking we saw some raccoons. One of them was quite a young one. Johnnie talked to it and whistled at it, and it came right up to us. It kind of made our day. Anything like that makes your day when you are hunting, because it can be a long, lonely day if you don't see something happening.

On another one of our hunting trips into the Sayward area we decided to split up. Johnnie and Fred went around on the far side of a cedar swamp, while Nick and I hunted on the side nearest the road. They were to circle around and come back toward us when we got to the end of the road.

They went down in a little valley with a stream in it and we were on a road further over. We could see them way down there and saw a bunch of deer running in front of them. It was an old cedar swamp. When they logged they used to leave them, and I guess they're still there today. They are a help for the deer because every time we got deer, it seemed, they came out of the cedar swamps or ran into them.

While Nick and I waited for the others we had walked back to the truck and brought it up to the end of the road. This was my old half-ton Chev truck that I inherited with the Swanson sawmill in 1951. That was my first vehicle and the only one I had until about 1953 or so. It served the purpose.

Nick and I were sitting drinking a beer. It was super hot this day, about eighty degrees. We were sitting there with no shirts on, enjoying the view when we saw a bear down below us. It came through a bunch of alders, willows and cedars, and onto a big log across the creek, right below Nick and I. We fired a few shots at it and it fell over, but its claws stuck in the log and it hung there, in the air.

Fred and Johnnie got close to us about an hour later and yelled up the hill, "Hey, what were you guys shooting at?" Nick and I were on about the third beer by this time, drinking them hot because we didn't have an ice box.

I yelled at Johnnie to walk over a bit. "There's an uprooted tree there. Do you see it, that big fir? You can walk across the creek on it." It was the one with the bear hanging off it.

"Yeah, I see it," he said. Johnnie was in the lead and when he broke through the alders here was this bear, about ten or twelve feet ahead of him, with its paw across the log, dead. "Big bear! Big bear!" he shouted.

"Hey Johnnie, don't shoot, it's dead," I yelled before he could begin firing. The four of us went down and got it. We cut a pole and tied the bear under it. Then we packed it up to the truck and I gutted it. I couldn't believe the amount of twelve to fourteen inch worms in it. I never saw so many worms in something's stomach in my life. How that bear could have been so fat, I don't know. It had to be feeding a couple of hundred worms.

We tied the bear on the front fender and headed back to where we were staying, the Rainbow Auto Court in Campbell River. The next morning we were highballing back up toward Camp Five, with the bear still tied on the front fender. We were bouncing along the road in the dark up past the pulp mill when the rope on the bear broke where it was tied back to the door of the truck. When the rope broke the bear went forward and the front wheel ran over it. We ended up in the ditch, bear and all. We were pretty brassed off about that, as we had a dinged up fender. I said to hell with this bear. We cut the rope off, threw the bear in the bush, and carried on with our hunting.

By three o'clock in the afternoon we had a two point and a four point, so we were happy about that. We finished off that trip and came back home again. Another Ha! Ha! Ha! down the road, in the ditch and out, and a ruined bruin.

Around that time truck logging opened up the Northwest Bay, Ladysmith and Nanaimo Lakes areas, so we packed up our hunting in the North Island.

In 1954 I went hunting up at Northwest Bay on the opening of the deer season. They had people on the gates for years at most of these logging camps and could count the number of deer shot. The weekend of November 11th they opened up the doe season, and over 400 does, fawns and bucks came out of that one area. Today, I can assure you, they don't even get forty. You don't shoot the babies and the mommies if you want to have deer in the future. The game department always says they are going to have bigger and better deer. You look anywhere on Vancouver Island, where all those does have been shot, the deer got smaller and smaller; they haven't got bigger and bigger.

It was the same old story when I hunted in the Fernie, Elko and Cranbrook area. When they started talking about shooting does there the Fish and Game Clubs all opposed it. There were signs nailed on the trees up there—"Don't shoot the whitetail does or fawns, or you won't have any deer in the years to come." At the Nanaimo Fish and Game Club, some of us called these people the "Bambi shooters," and they still are as far as I am concerned.

The majority of members in the Nanaimo Fish and Game Club were all for shooting does and fawns. I was dead against it and it was one of the reasons why I quit going to the meetings. I tried to put a motion on the floor about stopping it, but there was only myself and one or two others out of about fifty of those guys who voted for it. My friend and I packed up our bags and out of there we went. I still go up there occasionally sports shooting, and my family and I still support the Club, but I am dead against their thoughts about shooting does and fawns.

6

I N THE EARLY 1950S, WHEN MOST MILLS started putting in barkers and chippers, I wanted to put a barker and chipper into the Brechin mill. Fred didn't agree with that; nor did some of the other relatives who had money in the company at the time. I decided then, to hell with you guys, and made the decision to build my own chipping plant.

In 1956, I built the G.W. Dorman Pulp Chip plant at 1840 Stewart Avenue, where the boat ramp and Public Market are today. I built most of the chip plant in my spare time, on weekends and at nights, as I was still working a full shift sawing at Brechin. I bought bark-free wood from Brechin Lumber and chipped it up for pulp chips. I was the first guy around this area to haul chips into the Harmac pulp mill. I was quite proud of this.

I also bought beachcomb logs for chipping. My old falling pal, Bill Adam from Nanaimo River Camp, was out of work, so he looked after the booming ground for me. We cut the logs into eight-foot lengths and I'd run them through a double head saw that cut them into seven-inch thick slabs. We ran these through a vertical edger we got from the Tahsis Company. I had it set so it cut seven-by-nines and dropped them into the chipper. We used to cut up those big logs in no time flat—into big chunks and whmmmm, into the chipper.

I got the chipper from M&B in Port Alberni. It was an old sawdust machine that they converted into a chipper. They had one just like it in Chemainus and it worked, so I thought I'd try it too. That was the main piece of machinery that I put into the mill.

I had a little eight-foot carriage mill that I cut the logs with. When I first got the carriage, I had to have a man on there to do the dogging. Then I made it automatic so that there was just one man who cut up all the logs to be fed into the chipper. This worked real slick. As a matter of fact, I had a lot of "big timers" come and look at that little chipping plant, which they thought was great. If they thought it was great, I guess it must have been okay.

Once I got the chipper plant running, I ran into a lot of trouble with Nanaimo's anti-noise by-laws. The people who lived in that area were always giving me hell. I don't know how many times I went to court. They used to call my chipper plant "The Monster" because when we threw wood in it, especially if we had dry, old wood on a clear night, you couldn't believe the noise that thing made as the wood rattled through the chipper. I guess it kept some people awake, but a lot of people who lived around there told me they couldn't sleep at night if it wasn't running, so there were various reactions to the noise.

And I had more than one angry word with my friend Jack Richardson next door at the Anchorage Marina. Sometimes, when we moved a boom in, we'd hit his floats and do some damage. We usually managed to work out a compromise. He always needed lumber and I needed to get my logs in—and bump them off his floats every now and again. I always fixed them, of course. We all got along down there in the end, but it took a few years.

When I first started the chipper plant there were several people squatting on the property and I had to get them off. One of them was a little old man, about eighty-four, who lived out over the water in a house on stilts. One morning when I came to work, he was floating in the water, dead. So that was the end of that squatter.

Beside him lived the Lewis lady. She had a couple of children, and her mother-in-law lived across the road. There was a float house tied up to the property that was owned by Walter Mearns. He raised a couple of girls and a son there. I had to get rid of all these squatters. It was very hard for me to send those people packing, especially the ones who had kids. But between the Harbour Commission and myself we finally got them out of there.

The fellow with the float camp was a fisherman. He towed his floats over to a little cove across from Brechin Point on Newcastle Island, and left it there all summer while he went fishing. When he came back he found people had broken in and stolen or smashed things. This turned him into a very bad enemy of mine because he figured I was to blame for all his problems.

He had a brother called Tightline Mearns, a great guy who did my towing until he died in 1959.

Less than two years after we had our first son, Shirley and I had another, Kevin, who was born March 21, 1957—the first day of spring. Shirley was a good mother, to our sons as well as my two daughters; and she was a super-hard worker. Although we were getting a bit crowded in our house on Wakesiah, we had a good time there.

One summer I built a small swimming pool for the kids in the back yard. We were having a barbeque one afternoon with our neighbors, the Fedjes, when I thought I'd play the clown to entertain everyone. The pool was only about three feet deep, and I'd built a slide going into it. I took one of the kids tricycle's up the slide and rode it down into the swimming pool. The end result of this was I wound up at the hospital and had eleven stitches put in my head. That wasn't too bad, but it kind of ruined the barbeque.

In 1957 the Brechin Lumber mill burned down. By then I had the G.W. Dorman Pulp Chip Company operating. I owned it outright. After the fire at Brechin Lumber, I added a sawmill to the chip plant. It took a lot of late nights and weekends to get the sawmill up and running. I spent a lot of money changing things around, and at the same time kept up a running battle with the neighbors, who we had all kinds of trouble with. But we got all that settled down and finally got things running smoothly.

I'm sure we could still be cutting logs there today if it hadn't been for the City of Nanaimo and people like Graham Roberts, the mayor at the time, who was always hounding me because I owed the city taxes. I often wonder how much in taxes they get out of that public market. It would be interesting to know. Anyway, that's the way it is.

After the Brechin mill burned down, I turned over all its assets to Fred. He renamed it, and operated it as a lumber yard, reman plant and planer mill on Dorman Road in North Nanaimo. About five years ago I bought the company back from him, and own it now as an operating company.

After I got the new sawmill going and got some export orders, I bought some lumber carriers from Hillcrest Lumber. When Hillcrest closed down they had an auction and I bought a bunch of stuff from them—a gang saw, an edger and a couple of carriers. I used them to haul lumber to the Assembly Dock. To get from the mill to the dock we had to travel through part of downtown Nanaimo, and we had more than one accident. No one was ever hurt, but we tied up traffic occasionally. It was usually a matter of a little lumber dropped while going through town. It would scatter all over the place, so I'd send a couple of boys down from the mill to help pick it up and the road would be blocked off for a while.

In those days, before logs were bundled, there were flat booms, and we used to have a lot of beachcombers. They used to have a field day. If they weren't "lend-leasing" the logs they were picking them off the beach or out of the water after a high tide.

There was an old beachcomber by the name of Robinson whose logs I often bought. He boomed up over on Newcastle, right by the dock. There were lots of booming grounds around there. One year I didn't buy many of his logs. I'd bought a boom at Nitinat from Crown Zellerbach, a two-section bundle boom of short, balsam logs. They were short, all sixteen to twenty-four footers. It went missing in March, and I couldn't figure out where it had gone.

In July, Robinson came over to the mill and asked me if I

wanted to buy a boom he had. When I went to look at them, there were my two sections of short, balsam logs mixed all through his twenty-four-section boom.

"I'll buy these logs off you," I said. Beachcombed logs all had to be sold through Gulf Log Salvage, which sent part of the money it got for logs to the original owners, whose numbers were stamped on the ends of the logs.

"Can't you just take some of these logs and cut them up?" He wanted to make a side deal, without going through Gulf Log Salvage.

"I tell you what I'll do," I said. "I'll take ten sections of those logs. I'll cut them up and pay you for them, instead of going through Gulf Log Salvage and wasting a lot of money."

I got the ten sections of logs and sawed them up. When Robinson came over to get his money, I said "I'm not paying you."

"How come you're not going to pay me?" he asked.

"I'll tell you why, Robinson. You stole those logs from me. I had two sections of bundles that went missing and I can show you more logs of mine all through those sections you have left. You're not getting paid for those ten sections. It's as simple as that. Or I'm going to charge you with stealing my logs." The old potlicker didn't know what to do. He said, in the end, "Okay." That was only one time I had logs stolen.

Another time I had a boom of real nice logs that came from Texada Island. Texada Logging used to sell me a lot of logs and I would get them towed over to Nanaimo by Chemainus Towing. This was a six-section bundle boom, which is a lot of logs, and it went missing. We couldn't find it and when we asked someone at the towboat company they said it had come loose and drifted out of the harbour.

"How come you guys know about it? Why didn't you do something?" I wanted to know.

"Oh, we were too busy to do anything about it," they said. "We think one of the beachcombers over at Protection Island has the boom." I got to the Forest Service and told them what happened, so they got in touch with Gulf Log Salvage, who gave me a big bloody bill for getting my logs back to me. They said they found the boom drifting out at Snake Island. It's just a crock that a boom could drift out of Nanaimo Harbour to Snake Island in the summertime without anyone seeing it. To this day I think some shady characters let that boom go so a beachcomber could get it.

In the mid-1950s I started hunting in Alberta, the first time in 1954 after being married in August. I took my father-in-law, Fred, and his brother, Willie, along on the first trip and most of the ones that followed. We always had a great time, and the farmers always enjoyed Fred and Willie because they understood how tough things were farming. They had moved from Saskatchewan after seven years of drought; said to hell with this noise, packed their bags and moved to Nanaimo where they got something happening. When I went hunting in Alberta I always made sure I had one of them with me when I asked for permission to hunt because they had the respect of the farmers.

The first trip to Alberta we shot pheasants and other upland game birds, as well as ducks and geese. We met a fellow named Jim Austin who put us up in a deserted old farm building. There were no lights or electricity, and grain was stored in part of the building. We put our sleeping bags on the floor and slept there. There were mice running over us, and sparrows up in the rafters shitting on us. That's what we called roughing it in the '50s.

The following winter I talked to Ernie Johnson, who owned Johnson's Hardware in Nanaimo, and he told me about goose hunting. He said he'd gone to a place named Cereal and there were lots of geese there. They'd had a pretty good time hunting, even though Ernie had stepped in a badger hole one night when they were packing out their geese in the dark and broken his ankle. He said to find some nice fields and watch for the geese in the morning. When you see them flying just follow them if you can. I went there in 1955 with Bob Malpass, Bill Gordon and the two flatlanders, Fred and Willie. We went to Cereal, and slept the first night in our sleeping bags on the concrete floor of a gas station. The owner was very nice to us. He had a little restaurant attached to the garage and one of the things we learned to look forward to every day was having one of the biggest T-bone steaks you ever saw for a dollar.

The next morning we were sitting along a road, watching for geese, when we saw a flock of about 300. We followed them along the highway for about fifteen miles, where they went into a farm, not far away from where we were staying at the gas station. Ernie had told me to spot the geese in the morning and pick a spot to hunt. If they are in there in the afternoon, he said, come back that night and dig pits to shoot from the next morning.

I went in to talk to the owner of the farm, who was a doctor that was very sympathetic to hunters. I asked him if we could pitch our tent just outside his gate, on the side of the road. He said, "Of course, if you want to stay there, go ahead." Later, when the geese were gone, we pitched our tent.

We watched the geese when they came back again later that day. When they took off we went over and checked where they had been feeding. Ernie had told us to find the last of their droppings. They fed into the wind and when they came back in the morning they would come into that spot. He told us to dig our pits there, at right angles to the wind. That night we went out, before even we thought about our dollar T-bones, and dug our pits.

The idea was to get a hole about three feet deep, big enough to crouch down in so the geese couldn't see you when they came in to land. It was sandy in this field, and easy to dig, so we really lucked out on our first pits in Alberta. Later, we found, it could take two or three hours of hard digging to make a pit.

On our second night we slept in our tent on the frozen ground, in the snow. I still had my Timothy Eaton sleeping bag, and my ass was frozen through and through. I decided I had to find a better place to stay.

The next morning before dawn we went out in the field and got into our pits. In came the geese, about ten feet off the end of our gun barrels. We ended up getting twenty-six of them, which made us all pretty happy.

When we were walking back to the car and thinking about something to eat, three geese flew toward us, quite high. Willie had some slugs, and he quickly put one in his shotgun. Somebody had told him to bring some slugs to fire at high flying geese and he might get one. "Hey, Will," I said. "Give them about eight feet of lead."

I don't know hom much lead he gave, but pow. One of the geese went into a big glide and down into a slough. Willie took his clothes off, waded out there and got that goose. He was plenty cold. It was the beginning of October and there was ice on the water. We went back to the restaurant and got him into some dry clothes.

Ernie had said that most often the geese would not come back to the same pits twice. But early in the season quite often they are stupid so we decided to try those pits one more time, that afternoon. We got eleven more. Bill Gordon got four snow geese; they were perfectly white. That's the only time we ever shot any. They were as big as the Canada geese if not bigger.

We loaded them all in the station wagon and went over to have our T-bone steaks. A fellow at the cafe was looking at our geese and spotted three of them with warts on their noses. We didn't know what they were.

"Holy Christ," he said. "You can't shoot them." They were Ross geese.

"Do you want them," I asked him.

"Yeah. I can take them home and get them plucked. Everybody knows I'm not a goose hunter."

So there we were on our first goose hunt with almost our limit in only one day's hunting. We didn't have much trouble getting the rest of them—and maybe a few more.

When I had talked to the doctor who owned the farm earlier in the day, he told me I could stay in the farm house. He didn't live on the farm, but a hired man stayed there. I got my Timothy Eaton bag, laid it out on an old couch in the house and slept there that night.

The next morning we went hunting pheasants around Brooks. It was the opening day of the season. We hunted on a farm owned by a fellow named Carson, near Duchess. The farmer worked in town, but he had this lovely farm with more pheasants on it than any place I ever saw. In later years, we had great control over hunting on that farm. I would phone him ahead of time, and as long as he owned that farm, nobody could hunt on it but us guys. I doctored him up with fresh spring salmon, cohoes and canned salmon, and took him and his wife out to dinner every year.

This morning, some of us were hunting on our own. Bill Gordon, Willie, and I all had our own dogs and were hunting separately with them. Bob came along with me and we shot five pheasants each. That's what we were allowed at the time. We came in and Bill had his five. I went over to pick up Fred and Willie, and they had seven. A total of twenty-two. In the afternoon we decided to go out again and, lo and behold, we picked up another thirteen. We finished up with thirty-five pheasants on the first day of pheasant season.

We came back to the doctor's farm during the day, and I went over to the house. The hired hand was armed with a shovel, trying to chase a skunk out of the house. I guess he wasn't using enough IQ. If he'd have left the goddamn door open the skunk probably would have left on its own. It was starting to warm up and was a nice sunny day.

The skunk was in beside the couch. The hired man went in with his shovel and took a couple of whacks at it. It sprayed all over my sleeping bag. I could not believe how much the cabin smelled of that skunk.

We got some tomato juice and washed the sleeping bag down as best we could. I stunk; everything stunk. But I wasn't going to sleep on that frozen ground again. I stayed in the cabin that night and one more night, skunk smell and all. It was enough to make anyone barf, but I managed to get through it.

We took all the geese and pheasants, as well as some ducks we shot, to a place in Brooks and had them plucked. Then we froze them and put them in an ice box in my new International Travelall. Bob Malpass, who was always in a hurry—his hunting span was good for about four or five days and then he had to get on to someting else—had left early with Bill Gordon, so I headed back to Nanaimo with the flatlanders.

When we got to Elko we were gassing up and asked the fellow at the service station if there was any good hunting around there. "There's a good mountain for deer down the road about ten miles," he said. "You just ask anybody when you get down there."

We were driving along and came across three boys riding

on a horse, a big plug of a horse. We stopped and I asked them where the mountain was. One of them said "That's it right there." I asked him if there were any deer up there.

One of the boys said "Oh yeah, there's lots of deer up there. I was up there with my .22 two weeks ago and I wounded one." I asked if people would mind if we hunted up there. "No," he said. "Nobody cares."

Fred and Willie decided they would hunt around the fields because they figured the deer would be feeding there. I told them I was going to head up the mountain. Everybody used to call me Mountain Climber around Nanaimo. I was the guy who always climbed the mountains and usually got the most deer.

Up that mountain I went until I realized it was getting dark, and started back down. I was coming down a draw and saw two whitetail bucks below me, a four-pointer and a five-pointer. They were eating and I got a rest on a little tree and let drive. Holy Christ, what did they do but came straight up the draw, running right toward me. They thought somebody was shooting at them from down below. It's always a good idea to be above the deer because it confuses them. One of them was limping badly and I figured I'd hit it. I waited until it was about forty feet from me and whapped it. The other one was to the left of it about ten feet, and I whapped it. Down they both went.

I realized I had to get the deer down off that mountain before it was dark. I didn't gut them, but grabbed one and dragged it down the draw. It was pretty easy going and, at that time, I was super strong. They were good sized deer. I got down to within hollering distance of the flatlanders, and they came over and gave me a hand. Willie said he'd gut the deer I'd dragged down and Fred came back up with me to find the other one. It was dark by this time and all we had was a two-cell flashlight with almost-dead batteries. We went back up the mountain and looked for that deer until almost ten that night. I even went back the next year to look for a skelton, and never found it. I figured it was dead, but I hadn't shot it again, or gutted it, so it might have got away. But, I'm not too sure we went back to the right spot either.

We loaded the deer into the Travelall and carried on. We couldn't wait around until the next day because we had all the birds in the car thawing out. We went off down the road very reluctantly, as far as I was concerned.

When we got home we hung the deer in Willie's barn. We were skinning it and noticed it was wounded in the front leg. I thought it was from my first shot. Instead, there was a .22 bullet right in the joint on the front leg. It was from the boy on the horse we'd met. I tried to find that boy the following year to let him know he had hit the deer, but I couldn't. I'd completely missed it when I shot at it the first time.

On another one of our Alberta hunting trips in the late '50s I was driving my Travelall. Bob Malpass was with me in the front and Bill Gordon was the number one drink maker in the back. We were in a hurry to find some geese, about 4:30 in the afternoon. We were lining up a goose shoot and we wanted to make sure we saw them when they came into a field. I was doing about eighty miles an hour along a flat prairie road when Bill said "Hey. There's a detour sign there."

"Holy fuck. And I know why there's one." I tramped on the gas. They were replanking a bridge and there were three four-by-twelves missing in one gap and two in another. I flew over the fucking bridge at about eighty-five miles an hour. We didn't even notice the planks were missing.

"I thought you were going to spill the drinks," Bill stuttered from the back seat. "Okay, son. Let's slow down now. Let's have a quick drink, before we really get into trouble."

In the fall of 1957 we were having a hard time getting ducks at Michael Lake because they didn't come in quite low enough, especially on a nice day. I decided we should make ourselves a tower. I got some of the boys—Johnnie, Andy and Sam Sebastiano — and we built a tower, thirty feet high, right in their flight path. We built a box on top of the tower that would hold three or four of us. It had a ladder up the middle and a trap door in the center of the floor. We fastened a bunch of brush on the top so, hopefully, the ducks would think it was a tree. It was just what we needed. After we got it up, our ratio of ducks to shells fired increased a lot. We managed to get ourselves a lot of ducks out of that tower. It stood there for three or four years. Then we had a big storm and the bloody thing blew over.

In the late '50s Johnnie and I decided to go up and do a bit of salmon fishing at Campbell River. We went to a place with old cabins on the beach, and boats to rent. The next day we went out fishing and caught some coho. Johnnie got a twenty-six-pound spring and, because we didn't have a club in the boat he had to kill it with his beer bottle. When we were headed back in to the dock the gas line broke. We managed to get back in but the guy who owned the place wasn't very happy with us.

The next morning we got ready to go out again. This fellow's boats were run into the water on a set of tracks, and a boat was sitting there, ready to go. Johnnie was putting our fishing rods, gear and lots of beer into the boat when the guy said to him, "Where do you think you're going?"

"For shit's sake," Johnnie said. "Can't you see those are fishing rods. They're not guns; we're not going bloody hunting."

"Yeah? And you're not going fishing in my boat if you're going to talk to me like that."

Johnnie gave him some more lip. I calmed Johnnie down and tried to get things smoothed over so we could use the boat. But do you think that potlicker would give us a boat? No goddamned way. So, we had no boat to go fishing that day. Johnnie's mouth did us out of that one. We spent most of the day in the bar and managed to line up another boat for the following morning. By noon on the second day we had seven cohoes and two good-sized springs, and were on the road home to Nanaimo. A good weekend of fishing.

In the 1950s we were allowed to fish at the mouth of Nanaimo River, right in front of the assembly docks, for the big spring salmon going up the river in late August. One year, in 1957 I believe it was, Sam Sebastiano was out fishing by himself and caught a forty-seven-pound spring. I told him I'd give him thirty dollars for it.

"What do you want do with it?" he asked me.

"I want to send it to my friend Jim Austin in Hilda, Alberta. He's been looking after me lately and we've been getting all kinds of good hunting down there in the fall. I want to send him a nice fish."

Sam agreed and sold me the fish for thirty dollars. Imagine that, a forty-seven-pound spring for thirty dollars. He brought the fish over to my house and gave me a hand pounding together a plywood box as quick as we could. We put in some dry ice and sent it off. According to Jim, it arrived in great shape. He owns a store there that has been in operation since 1893. That week all the people in Hilda got fresh salmon from him.

In the 1950s we had a pipe band in Nanaimo. They called it the Nanaimo Pipe Band. Being a little short on Scots in Nanaimo, the band was a pretty wild mixture of guys in kilts. Three-quarters of them were Italians, including Sam and Archie Sebastiano. Johnnie was in it, and Polish. I'm a bloody Irishman. We had all sorts of escapades. On one occasion we went to Bellingham for a parade. I was leading the parade and some girls ran along beside me, wanting to know what was under my kilt, lifting it up to have a look. After that, I thought I'd fool them, so I never wore any shorts. I don't know whether it was too small or too big, but the girls had a giggle when we appeared at the PNE, in Seattle and, once, in Hawaii.

One of the toughest things about being in the sawmill business is being responsible for other people. With all the machinery running, a sawmill can be a dangerous place, and I had my share of close calls, and more.

At G.W. Dorman Pulp Chip we had an A-frame to unload trucks. When a truck came in with a load of logs, we used it to lift off the logs and dump them in the water. When the tide was out they would pile up and were hard to work loose. One day, when I was working on the saw, we had quite a pile of logs, right up to the brow log. The fellow working on the boom was trying to pull the logs down, hoping they'd all slide out into the water. I was watching him when the whole pile came down at once. They were nice, uniform second-growth logs, twenty-six or twenty-eight feet long, and eight to twenty-four inches in diameter, so they rolled easily. He was trying to run up over the logs and stay on top of them, but they spread out, floating, and he fell down between them.

I stopped sawing and hollered to everybody to grab peaveys. There were twenty of us there in about two seconds flat. He was up to his armpits, trying to keep from going between the logs. If you ever fall between a bunch of logs like that, they will close over on top of you, trapping you underneath, and you drown.

I ran down and was dancing around on the super slippery logs. I didn't have caulk boots on so I fell on my butt a couple of times. I was scared I was going to fall in the water and get trapped like he was. I managed to grab on to him and the guys with peaveys were able to move the logs enough so we could yank him out. I thought he was a goner for sure when I saw it happening, but we managed to save his skin. It scared him so bad he quit a week later.

He went on to become a fisheries officer at Campbell River, although he had a drinking problem. He came over to Stuart Island one time and came up to me when I was tied up at the dock. "Dorman," he said. "If I catch you with more than your limit of salmon, I'm going to pinch you. I'm the boss now, not you."

"Look you drunken bum," I said. "I know you're pissed right now. If you want this job you better not be drinking on it, or you won't have one. I won't have to squeal on you; somebody else will. Besides, don't ever come on my boat or I'll throw you overboard." I never saw that idiot again. I should have let him drown.

Another friend of mine had a close call in an accident at that sawmill. This man's name was Joe Jones and he was about 72 or 73 years old. He worked on the boom, where we had a side lift that hoisted the logs out of the water, into the sawmill, and put them through the barker. I looked out the office window early one morning, and there was Joe, floating face down in the water. I figured he'd had a heart attack. I ran out of the office, down into the booming ground, and pulled him out of the water. He was half conscious.

I pumped the water out of him and he kind of came around a little. I picked him up, packed him into the first aid room, and put him on the bed. He came around and was happy as a clam. When I asked him what happened he sad he'd had a dizzy spell and fell in the water. "Well Joe," I said, "you'd better have a checkup so we can see what's wrong with you." We took him up to the hospital and checked him out. The doctors said he shouldn't work any more because he had a heart condition. He didn't last more than a year before he died.

I once hired an old fellow to work in the chipper plant who was Hungarian. He had left Hungary before the revolution, and he was looking for a job. I asked him, "Do you think you are tough enough to do this job?"

"Oh, yeah," he said, "I can do that job." He didn't speak very good English, but I gave him a job. He turned out to be a real hard working guy. One day a big knot flew out of the chipper and gave him a "Benny Hill" right on the side of the head. It took eleven stitches to patch him up, and I thought I'd better find somebody else to work in his place. I got another guy for the morning, and when I went to work there was this guy with a big patch on his head.

"How come you're at work with your banged-up head?"

"I tell you what," he said, "If I stay home, it hurts more than it does at work. When I'm at work I don't have time to think about the pain. I want to work."

A few days after I hired the Hungarian fellow, another guy came along looking for a job. I looked at him and he was the scrawniest looking guy I'd ever seen. "Do you think you could do a day's work, you scrawny bastard?" I was kind of sarcastic in those days.

"Hey, I'm tough as rat shit and twice as nasty," he said. "Sure I can work. No problem." I gave him a job and he was the best worker I ever had at Brechin Lumber or the chip plant. His name was Alfie Ives. Besides being a good worker, he had a few brains. When I built my chipper plant, he worked nights and weekends with me, after working in the sawmill all day. He ran the barker and did millwright work, and before long he was a favourite of mine.

On one occasion, I was sawing and the big, thirty-inch wide belt that took the lumber from the head saw was wandering on the head pulley. There was an adjuster on the pulley, and Alfie reached in to tighten it. He had on a raggedy old T-shirt, ripped to hell. Somehow the T-shirt caught on the pulley and belt. It slammed his whole body into the head pulley. If there had been a bigger motor on it, I'm sure it would have torn his head off. The pulley was slipping on the belt, and Alfie was stuck in there with his neck bent back. I thought for sure his neck was broken.

I always carried a pocket knife that was super sharp. I grabbed it, and with one slash, cut that thirty-inch belt, three-quarters of an inch thick, from side to side. It flipped over, and Alfie flopped onto the floor, unconscious. We got him on a stretcher and he came around, wanting to know what had happened. I told him and said "We're taking you up to the hospital. You've got either a broken arm or a broken neck, you silly bastard. What's wrong with you?"

"Well," he said, "I don't know." He lay on the stretcher a bit and thought about it. He moved his arm, which was skinned to hell. "I don't think there's anything wrong with that."

"How about your neck?" I asked him. He wiggled it around.

"I think it's okay."

"Can you stand up?" I asked him.

"I don't know. Why don't you give me a hand." So a couple of us got him on his feet. He shook himself like a raggedy-tailed dog and thought about it for a while. "I think I'm okay." And the bugger was. He had a coffee and came back to work, helping fix the belt.

About a month later I bought a lot of peeler cores from Victoria Plywood. They bundled them up in booms and sold them. In with the peeler cores were split logs and other odd pieces of junk wood that were hard to handle.

I was only chipping at the time because the lumber market was down and there wasn't much money in sawmilling. Because things were slow I decided to go off hunting in Alberta for a few days. I put Alfie in charge of the plant and on the day we left I went down to make sure he had everything under control. "Do you think you can handle these peeler cores?" All we were doing was cutting them small enough to get them in the chipper.

"Oh, yeah," he said. He was out on the steel deck, at the top of the jack ladder that brought logs up to the mill from the water. It had a big, heavy duty Star roller, about ten to twelve inches in diameter, with big, sharp spikes sticking out of it to grip the logs. Alfie was wrestling with a junk log right beside the Star roller, that was still running. I said to him, "If you ever slip on that steel deck and get your foot in that roller, you're going to know all about it. Don't do that. Blow three whistles to get the millwright to help you." Alfie said the guy wouldn't come and help, and it was easier to do it himself.

I caught the Blackball ferry and headed for Alberta, along with my friend, Harold Mayovsky, who was my office manager, and Terry Rodway. When we got to Brooks, we checked into a motel and started hunting Monday morning. At 1:30 the next morning there was a knock on the motel door. I answered it and as soon as I saw it was a cop the first thought that came into my mind was that something had happened to Alfie.

"You've had a bad accident at your sawmill."

"Is it Alfie Ives?"

"Yes."

"Is he dead?"

"Yes." He told me what had happened, which was just what I had warned Alfie about. I was in a panic. We had a little snort and talked about it. There was nothing I could do to get any more information from Brooks, so I decided to get back to Nanaimo. I phoned up my good friend Jack Resseller, who lived in Brooks, to see if I could bum a car off him.

"Oh yeah, you can have my car," he said. "I've got to go to Calgary so I can pick it up. You just leave it at the airport."

I got the first plane out of Calgary Tuesday morning and when I got into Nanaimo the mill was closed, so I went to see the RCMP. They showed me pictures of the accident. I could not believe that a man could be mangled so badly. His right arm was completely missing, torn off at the shoulder. I figured he had grabbed something, or done something to try and save himself. His left foot had got caught in the roller, and then got his other foot was dragged in. His heart was hanging out of the bottom of his rib cage. The left arm was still there but there was no more body left. It was all gone. They were the most horrible pictures I ever saw in my life. It took a long time for all of us at the mill to get over it, and we didn't start work until the following week.

In 1959 the IWA was on strike for fifty-nine days, so I spent that summer building a house at Long Lake. To help me, I hired four fellows who worked in the chipper plant. Although I didn't have any money, I paid them the same wage as they got in the plant, and they held off getting their money until Christmas.

We worked all day, and at five or five-thirty I went home, had my dinner, and came back at six-thirty or seven with my friends Sam Sebastiano and Johnnie. We worked until around eleven o'clock, then went over to the Wellington and had a few beers, if we didn't have them with us, then went home. I put in super long hours, and we managed to finish the house and move in by late October.

We had a lot of fun there, with nail driving contests and that sort of thing. Don MacDonald did the electrical work. When he was a young lad he had it in for me. While I was living at 265 Pine with my in-laws and building my house on Wakesiah, we were sitting in the living room playing bridge one night, and a rock came flying through the window. I looked out and saw this kid running down the road toward Fitzwilliam. I had my slippers on and I was plenty fleet footed in those days. I chase this guy up Fitzwilliam, down the next street, and caught up to him about half way down the block. I recognized him from the Catholic church. I kicked his ass, then I walked him home and told his mother. Somehow the window got fixed.

He was only a young lad, fourteen years old, and he kind of had it in for me after that. When he was older we happened to meet one night in Chinatown. This was a great haunt for us fellows in the '50s, and we went to the Wong's place a lot for meals. One night he was there. He was quite a bit younger than me and he decided we were going to have a punch up, and I got the worst of it. He outweighed me by about twenty pounds, and was six foot two tall.

It wasn't much later when we had another fight, and I got the best of him. He didn't like that too much and wanted to have a third encounter. By this time I was maybe 185 or 190 and he was up to about 220. We went at it and I uncled him again.

When I started the house at Long Lake he came to me and said "Hey, Dorman. I'm not working much right now. Why don't I wire your house for you?" He'd become an electrician.

"Good idea, Don," I said. After that we became great pals and worked together helping kids in sports—softball and that sort of thing. Our sore heads and black eyes were all forgotten long before he died a few years ago at a young age. That was too bad, but I was happy we'd made up before he died.

George Dorman with whitetail deer in East Kootenays, 1968.

Ken Olsen, George Dorman and Ken's neighbour, with salmon
caught at Stuart Island, 1968.

Reg Dorman (l), Brian Dorman and Jerry Mutter with Springs caught at Stuart Island, 1968.

Children from the Dorman, Stanbrook, Giese and McGillvery families camping at Rebecca Spit on Quadra Island, 1969.

George Dorman duck hunting at Jenner, Alberta, in 1970. This photo was used on the cover of a U.S. hunting magazine.

Hunting geese at Jenner, Alberta, in 1971. Randy Dorman (l), Randy Giese, Fred Judson, Willie Judson, Harlen Giese, "Jim," Tim Dorman (front), George Bajich, Brian Dorman, Frank Bajich and Kevin Dorman.

Brian (l), Kevin and George Dorman in 1971 with trophies from trap shooting competition at Nanaimo Fish & Game Club.

George Dorman (l) and Johnnie Bohoslowich at Bamfield in 1971 with George's 20-foot Rennel.

George Dorman and George Louie with 21 and 23 pound Coho at Rivers Inlet, 1971.

The G.W. Dorman Pulp Chip mill just before it was torn down in 1985.

Mill rent hike
sparks squabble

A Nanaimo alderman has criticised a local businessman for criticising council.

Ald. Nelson Allen Monday attacked George Dorman, owner of the Stewart Avenue sawmill, for comments he had made on a decision of council to increase the rent on the Dorman property.

Council had voted to increase the rent to $9,132 per year, on Allen's recommendation.

Dorman immediately afterwards announced he would have to layoff over 20 people and placed much of the blame on the rent increase.

However, Allen said the layoffs are not as a result of the price hike but were already pending before the city made its announcement.

"But somehow we are blamed. Dorman apparently goes through this ritual each time his rent goes up."

At this point in the meeting Mayor Frank Ney suggested Allen shouldn't be slandering

people to which the alderman replied that he objects to Dorman's complaint that he (Allen) was sticking his nose into other people's business with the rent hike, when the property is owned by the city.

He said the two-and-a-half-acre site Dorman is using could be worth as much as $1.3 million if the city was to sell it and that with such a value, the rent should be as much as $8,472 per month.

The increase said Allen, had also been agreed to by Dorman and his mill manager in discussions with properties director Ted Anderson, prior to any announcement being made.

The alderman's comments came after council approved another rent increase — this time to Simpsons Sears for a 807 square foot property on Cameron Road. The lot is used as a loading bay.

The rent will increase to $870 per year effective March 1, 1978, from the current $400 per year charge.

Dorman slams IWA's Munro

Sir:

I find Jack Munro's taking the IWA out on strike in July very bad timing, considering there was an election due in October (the exact date was not known at the time, but it was clear an election would be held fairly soon after the Socred leadership convention) . . . and knowing that we had a lumber tariff facing us of 15-36 per cent per cent. (He says there will be no loss of jobs if we have to add this tariff to the price of lumber, which is between $250 and $350 per thousand boardfeet, delivered, in the U.S.).

Try applying 15-36 per cent onto this lumber and who is going to buy it? He stated more than once on television that there won't be one job loss if this happens. Wake up Jack Munro. Some Canadians may be a little thick, but I am sure the Americans are not!

The timing of the strike brought on by Jack Munro and his associates (mainly Jack Munro) jumped the gun, probably as a result of the criticism from the union about his 1985 get-together (and that Kelowna Accord) with Bill Bennett, and leading the boys to restraint and little or no increases in wages.

After the criticism of this accord, he thought he would show the industry he would be much tougher in '86, forgetting the election and the tariff. He blew it! And, with his "bloody" and "damns" and half-assed loggers' language, I have noticed that he learned three new words — "lunacy," "insanity," and "idiotic."

I think it is about time that the IWA (with no further backing from the IWA in the U.S.) found themselves a new leader, probably who would have more thoughts of leadership than to have his members on this lengthy, ill-timed strike.

A proper military leader would not lead his members against two tanks (a 15-36 per cent tariff and an election) both known to Munro at the time of taking strike action with a handful of troops.

I hope the IWA members, wives and children remember this "idiotic" time to strike when they see their empty stockings and lack of Yuletide cheer, and I hope they place the responsibility on their leader.

I think it is high time that wives had more to say than their husbands, who at times may think it's fun to be on strike. At different times this summer and fall, I have travelled around and seen the picket lines in the forest industry. I noticed all summer long that the boys always had beer on the hood of their vehicles, or in their ice boxes and were having a great laugh at the companies they were on strike against. I also noted in my hunting adventures that the beer was becoming non-existent, and finally, when it came down to October and November I noticed coffee thermoses. I wonder after their present vote (rejecting the Hodgson Report), if they even have coffee? I hope so.

Letters

The best timing for a strike would have been when the election was decided, but more important when the percentage of the tariff was pinned down, so that the industry knew where it stood; and there probably could have been a lot more benefits.

Who, in their right mind, would ever give in to a union and its whining, when they don't know where this 15-36 per cent begins and finishes?

As far as I am concerned, a major problem is the amount of timber licences held by the big companies, who control most of the timber on this coast and in the interior, and who pay around 10 cents to $4 per metre (averaging 70 cents), when people like myself, and the small loggers, pay the government up to $33-34 per metre on government timber sales.

I think the final tariff should be slapped against all these cheap timber licences held by the large and small companies in B.C. — so that all this money stays in B.C. is used in reforestation to supply jobs, instead of being taken by the Americans in the form of tariffs. And, Jack, your IWA members will still lose jobs — granted.

I have no beefs about the contracting-out clause, but most timber licences, when they were granted, had written in by the government that 50 per cent of the timber on these licences had to be contracted out to the small logger . . . no mention of the small IWA logger.

Some of the things that annoy the big companies include: fallers getting $275 per day; excessive waste of gas and the fact that, at times, two fallers work together, with one working for three hours, while the other babysits until they change about.

Production is so low in the big companies that when they contract out, the contractors are producing wood for one half the cost, as they have more discipline over their loggers (fallers either produce or leave the site).

Loggers who lose their IWA job normally get jobs with the contractors who are doing the contract-out work. The only difference working for these contractors is that their "dog days" are over. They are not working for the companies any more.

One thing about the men working in the sawmills, they do a good eight hours work per day and much credit to the green chain boys . . . they have to either pile that lumber or eat it. They always have it piled.

Regarding sawmills, there is nothing wrong with contracting out millwright work or alterations during shut downs, since most millwrights are incapable of this type of work. Most millwrights now get a ticket if they can fix a bicycle chain.

The big companies want the logger to work 10 hours per day for a 4-day week (40 hours) and they want production to be on a seven-day schedule, at straight time. Meanwhile, millwrights normally work a full year, while loggers work for perhaps eight months a year. It's the loggers who should get the time and a half for Sunday, not the millwrights.

The loggers and the big companies who only log eight months per year and have more than one piece of machinery that costs over $1 million have to, and should be able to use that machinery more than 40 hours per week, to suit production requirements.

I am a well-versed and educated man in the industry, having been in the sawmill and logging business for 35 years and experiencing such wonderful times with PPWC and IWA workers. I worked in the industry from 1942 on — less time served in the Canadian navy. Out of Cowichan Lake came the union 'IWW' (I Won't Work!) They were lead by a bunch of CCF and communist organizers.

Jack Munro and associates tried to break up FIR, by allowing any company that was willing, to sign a contract for no further contracting out.

One third of their 30,000 workers and some of the companies signed this contract. He was looking for more. In the meantime, he split the ranks and it is no wonder, when the vote was put up to accept the government report that the working members (one third) voted overwhelmingly by 93 per cent to reject the Hodgson report.

Who would not do that, in the face of a fat Christmas turkey in front of them, when they know that their pals, who also voted by a lesser majority for rejection, don't have a fat future and turkey, in front of them?

"I feel these 10,000 workers are trying to save face in front of their striking comrades. I say, further, it is another Munro screw-up.

"United we stand, divided we fall." May we in the end stumble together.

If you want to work — go to work! If you don't — stand up and voice your opinions and get out and vote. Don't sit around home and complain.

Don't be influenced or railroaded by a few militant union agitators and loudmouths who are moonlighting outside the industry. (I am sure we could all quote many names.)

Where is the spirit of the proud Canadians who built this country? Workers, stand up and show that great Canadian spirit and speak out for what you feel is right providing that you are a proud Canadian and believe in your families and well-being . . . come forward and act like one, because you don't listen to a bum leader (loggers' terminology)!

George W. Dorman,
Box 16, Terrien Road,
RR1, Nanoose

Andy Poje at China Creek in 1991.

Johnnie Bohoslowich with Rainbow trout from pond at George Dorman's Craig Bay house.

George Dorman with Jim Luckhurst and a 47-pound Spring salmon
at Langara Lodge, 1989. Jim died January, 1993.

Sam Sebastiano with a
Spring salmon at China
Creek, 1991.

Johnnie Bohoslowich (l) and George Dorman with Spring salmon at
Knight Inlet, 1992.

George's dog Giggie at the Nanaimo Rocky Point house, 1991.

Fred (l) and Willie Judson (r), the Flatlanders, with George Dorman at his Rocky Point house, 1993.

7

IN THE EARLY 1960S, REVENUE CANADA DECIDED a lot of people around Nanaimo had too much money, so they thought they would check up on some of us. They raided people's homes and businesses, looking for anything they could find that was not right.

A Victoria revenue man named McGee organized a stake-out of the Dormans. There were twenty-six income tax people and mounties, with McGee running the operation over the radiophones from a command center they set up in the Malaspina Hotel. They came down on us all at once, my two brothers and myself. They had teams of revenue people and mounties that came to all of our homes and businesses, all at the same time. We were invaded by all these turkeys armed with search warrants, and they had a great time.

At that time I had the biggest home of all the Dormans. I was living at Long Lake, where there were a lot of workshops, playhouses and other buildings full of junk. They turned every-thing upside down without finding anything. What trapped me was an old friend, a Nanaimo policeman by the name of Cla-houn. He was a bit of a boozer and used to do a lot of drinking with Bob Malpass, Bill Gordon and myself.

I'd built a house on a float for Malpass down behind the Nanaimo arena, on the old Madill site. I built it for him in exchange for some logs, and he towed it over to Sechelt. Four revenue guys and Clahoun were searching my office when I remembered a piece of paper describing the deal between Bob and I that was in my desk drawer. When the income tax guys went into another part of the office, Clahoun stayed behind and stood looking out the window towards the booming grounds. I grabbed the piece of paper out of the drawer and stuffed it in my shirt pocket. It made a bit of noise, and Clahoun turned around and saw me, and asked me to give it to him. He called in the revenue boys and gave it to them.

That paper said the house was worth $10,000, and had been exchanged for that much in logs. In the end they charged me tax on the house, at the going rate plus penalties. Altogether, between my brothers and myself, I think they got close to $50,000. I wasn't too happy about that, and figured that one way or another I'd get it back. I did.

One Sunday, on the first day of the 1963 deer season, I was hunting down at the Judson farm on Michael Lake. Late in the afternoon I noticed a big five-point standing in the field. It was quite a long shot, but I gave it a pow, and down it went. We all headed for the truck to drive up and get it. As I was getting in the truck the deer got up and ran off into the bush. We took the dogs and went after it, but all we found was a chunk of meat the size of a hamburger. We never did find that deer. I was back there again on a Sunday in late November, and saw a big buck walking along the edge of the bush. Holy crow, I thought, what a deadly deer. I got my rifle and, Pow, down it went. We jumped in the truck and got the deer, took it down to the barn and hung it up to skin it. When we skinned the hide off it we noticed it had a real bad wound in the back leg. Then we realized it was the deer I had shot a couple of months earlier. Hair had grown over the wound, which was full of pus balls. I guess it was still fighting the shock of the bullet hitting it. It shows how tough deer are. If it had survived the winter it would have been good and healthy by spring.

After I married Shirley, when our boys started growing up, we all went hunting quite a bit together in Alberta. The first time we went down there with Brian he was only four years old. The three of us were staying in a trailer on a farm. We lined up a goose hunt with the farmer, and got seventeen geese. Later that day I ran into the farmer and he said, "Hey, down in the pond down there at my water hole, there's a bunch of wounded geese; at least five or six of them. You should go get them." We went down to the pond with a boat and got two of them.

I remembered that spot, and the following year I went back there with my friend, Terry Rodway. We shot in the same field with the farmer, who said there were some more geese in the same pond. We had no boat this time, but I had my red golden retriever and a black Cocker spaniel.

Most of the pond was frozen, except for a small area in the middle that the geese kept open by swimming around. There were a couple of geese on the ice, and the dogs ran out and brought back a one apiece. There were three more geese out in the water, and the dogs went out again. When the ice started cracking badly, the golden retriever came back. I called the Cocker spaniel back, but it wouldn't come. He kept on going out onto the thin ice after a goose, and the two of them went through the ice. The goose flopped his way back onto the ice and got away from the dog. The poor dog couldn't get back on the ice, and was swimming around, whining.

The farmer's hired hand was with us, and said, "I'll get that dog. There is a snow fence over there; with some old slab lumber for making ties for the fencing." He pulled a couple of boards off and used them like skis to go out on the ice. He got close to the dog and I hollered to him, "Can you swim?"

"No," he said. "I can't swim."

"Well, you're not drowning over my dog, come on back here." He didn't want to come back. The dog was whining and starting to go down. It bobbed up and down in the water, the poor thing. The hired man gave up, and by the time he got back to us the dog had gone under the water for the last time and drowned. That was one of the saddest things that ever happened to one of my dogs. That dog was such a great pheasant dog. He had a great nose. He wouldn't pay attention and stay back when you told him, but he could sure rout out cock pheasants. I shot a lot of pheasants with the help of that black Cocker spaniel.

On another trip to Alberta in the late 1960s we went to a Thanksgiving weekend turkey shoot in Brooks. It was a hot day for that time of year. When we got there we ran into some high rollers from Abbotsford and some of their friends, who arrived about noon in a big, new Cadillac.

About 3:30 that afternoon I was showing one of them my dogs that were in their cage in the back of my Travelall. "Let me show you my German shorthair," he said. "They're great duck retrievers."

"Yeah, I've heard about them," I said. "My friend had one and it was so afraid of the water it wouldn't even get its balls wet."

"I'll show you," this guy said, and opened up the trunk of his Cadillac.

"You've got three dogs, alright," I said. "But they're all dead. It's eighty degrees out here, you stupid bastard. What are you doing keeping dogs locked in a trunk all day." He took one look and slammed down the trunk lid. He went and picked up his friends and they went back to Tilley, where they had rented the top floor of the hotel. He got a backhoe, dug a hole and buried his dogs, and they went home.

A couple of years after this, I was hunting in Alberta with the two flatlanders, my inlaws Fred and Willie Judson, along with Bill Gordon and Bob Malpass. Bob, Bill and I had just finished some bird hunting on a farm about ten miles out of Brooks. It belonged to a man and his wife, who we called Duchess Mary because she was always dressed fit to kill. Their farm had some coulees on it where we used to get a lot of pheasants.

On this day, we were dropping in to say hello to her and her husband, and have a little snort with them. As we drove toward the farm, we were listening to the World Series on my truck radio. Somebody hit the ball just as we were driving into the yard, but we didn't hear what happened because the radio went all to hell with static. After Malpass and Gordon got out, I got my 12 gauge and put a magnum in it. "I'll fix that radio," I said to myself, and blew it to rat shit.

I had forgotten there were a bunch of blasting caps in the glove compartment, and in the back there was more than half a case of stumping powder we were using to blow out goose hunting pits. When I shot the radio, the glove compartment door flew open. I thought, Oh shit, this whole thing's blowing up in my face. For a brief moment I figured that was the end. Fortunately for me, those caps didn't go off.

The following year, 1966, I was in Alberta hunting again with my friends Malpass and Gordon, and my sons Kevin and Brian. They were quite young at the time. Most friends of mine didn't like kids along on hunting trips, but I wasn't about to let that bother me. They are my kids and I'm going to look after them the way I see fit. And, anyway, I'm the guy that organized the deal and got everything tickety boo.

The first night we were out blasting pits. We'd got a little more modern now, and were using electric blasting caps and a plunger. Even the powder was better. Instead of stumping powder we got a different kind. We could set up all the pits and blow them all at once. We dug the hole first with a post hole auger, set up the powder with a cap, and buried it in the hole. We did this late at night, drinking rum and coke.

I got a little fed up this night. It ended up that the only ones helping me were my sons, while the others were sitting back in the truck drinking and talking. We had met two American hunters that day and they were there as well. When we went to set the charge off it wouldn't go. I disconnected all the wires from the plunger and started tracking down the problem. I sent my kids back to the truck. "You don't know what's going to happen," I told them.

I yelled up to the truck. "One of you idiots come and give me a hand. I don't see why my kids should be checking out why this charge won't go off."

There was a big American there, a Marine veteran. He was a happy old guy, so he came down to give me a hand. "Well George, you know what people say about Americans. 'Fools come rushing in.' What do you want me to do?" I told him to start checking the wires to see why the charge didn't go off. We found the main wire was disconnected from the leads. We hooked it back up, hooked it up the plunger and gave it the plunge. Whap. Off it went. The next morning we got thirty-four geese. It turned out to be a pretty good shoot after all.

The Americans were both Korean war vets—big, tough guys who had their own motor home. That night we were staying at the Circle W Motel, and they had their motor home parked outside. We were sitting in it drinking, and they had loud music on. I guess we were all making quite a bit of noise because the fellow who owned the motel came out. He opened the motor home door and gave one of the Americans shit for all the noise we were making. The American jumped out and knocked the stuffing out of him.

I got out and settled things down. We had two rooms in the motel and I was worried about a place to stay. The owner got so mad at us he threw us out of there, so we had no rooms that night. We stayed in the motor home. It was pretty crowded with an extra five of us in there. The next day we drove up to Bassano, about thirty-five miles from Brooks, and found another place. Like the American said: Fools rush in. He rushed out and punched that guy and we were out on our ears. We had a good pheasant hunt after that, and I never saw the Americans again.

Another year, when Terry Rodway, Harold "Bookie" Malovsky and I were hunting in Alberta, a big storm came up. The wind was blowing so bad we couldn't hunt in the fields so we went down along the river in the coulees and hunted pheasants. The following day the sun came out and it was a beautiful day so we thought we'd drive down through the field again and hunt some more pheasants.

In the fall in Alberta, before the irrigation was turned off for the year, the farmers flooded their fields. The bottom end of this field was flooded. Bookie was driving and didn't see the water until it was too late. He was a little slow on the draw and we got stuck just awful.

We poured a snort and thought about it. There was a farm away off in the distance, a mile or a mile and a half away. I noticed there was a field that wasn't cultivated so I thought I'd take my dogs and hike over to the farm. I might even get a pheasant. That was the best idea I had, because I got two cock pheasants on the way.

I explained the situation to the farmer, and he came down and hooked onto us. After he towed us out, Terry drove. He took over the wheel and away we went. And what did he do? Drove into another flooded area. The water was hard to see in the stubble, so we were stuck again. We blew the horn like crazy at the farmer. He came back, hooked onto us and pulled us out again.

I took over the driving and banned the other two guys to the back seat where they sat, laughing like crazy. We lucked out and got a couple of pheasants along the road just before dark on the way into Brooks. It was another down the road we go, ha ha ha. The afternoon turned out not to be too bad after all, even though we did get stuck. Getting stuck in Alberta's muddy fields is the story of my life.

When I first started hunting in Alberta, it was in an area near Hilda, close to Bristol, Saskatchewan. There is a big area of sand dunes there, about twenty-two square miles of sand dunes. When we hunted prairie chickens there we always had good hunting. The thing that amazed me was how many deer there were in the dunes. They were mostly whitetails, but there were also lots of big mulies.

One time when we were hunting there a farmer told me there hadn't been a deer season in that area for ten years. But, he said, it was going to be opening up pretty soon. I said, "You let me know when it's opening up."

He did that, and when the deer season opened up, I was hunting pheasants in Brooks. I thought, "Well, I'll go down there and without a problem, I should be able to get a deer."

I went out with the farmer on a Saturday, and late in the afternoon a blizzard blew up. I saw a big whitetail buck with a doe. I took aim and let drive at the buck. It bolted. It was snowing so bad and the wind was blowing so hard you couldn't see where it went. The farmer thought he knew where it had gone, so we circled around, but we couldn't even find the tracks. There was about six inches of snow. We never found it.

I went back the following year with the farmer. We went back to the same spot and he found the skeleton of that buck. It had the biggest set of whitetail horns that I ever saw. I brought them home and they are in my rumpus room today. Those deer horns look like moose horns, they have such wide blades on them.

On another trip to Hilda, when Brian and Kevin were a bit older, they came along with Shirley and I. We were hunting prairie chickens in the area where all the deer were. I had a single shot twenty gauge which was given to me by Hammy Bailey, who owned Chemainus Towing and did a lot of towing for me. He had trained his three sons on this gun. After they went up to bigger guns, he said one day, "George, I'll give you this gun." I trained all my boys with that same gun. Brian has it to this day, and now he is training his own son on it.

On this occasion, Kevin had the gun and was beside me. Shirley and Brian were further over with Jim Austin, who at that time was the Mayor of Hilda. I said to Kevin, "Look at that big buck." It was a big six or seven point mule deer. It was laying in the sand behind some wild rose bushes, not more than forty yards away. Kevin up and gave it a whap with the 20 gauge. That deer took off like you couldn't believe.

When she saw what had happened, Shirley came storming over and chewed him out real good. Then she gave me shit for not stopping him. She told Kevin, "You go sit in the truck!" Poor Kevin had to sulk off with his gun and wait in the truck. It was about an hour or so before dark, so he didn't have to sit there too long. I guess he had a few thoughts about that big buck because he still gets excited when he sees one.

Later in the year, Jim was hunting with his pals on the opening day of the deer season, and ran into that same buck and shot it. At Christmas he sent me a Christmas card, and in it were a bunch of 7.5 pellets he had taken out of the hide of the deer. "One thing about your kid," he wrote. "He hit it." He mounted that deer and it's in his store today.

I went back to Hilda again shortly after that. This time I didn't have Shirley or my boys with me. Model 1100 Remington auto-loaders were the gun of the day, and Willie Judson and I each got one. We were hunting with my Travelall. Willie was in the back left hand seat, I was in the front left hand seat. Jim

Austen was in the front right and his friend, Wilbur, was behind him. Wilbur was only interested in drinking beer, not shooting.

There was a storm brewing, and the wind was really powerful. We hardly ever got out of the truck. Willie had his automatic out one window, and I had mine out another. That day we ended up shooting sixty-four Hungarian partridges, which wasn't bad in a fifty-five mile per hour wind storm. Later in the day, we went out to hunt prairie chickens and shot our limit. That was one of the best days we ever had hunting in that area. Earlier, we'd been hunting pheasants near Brooks and thought we'd drop by Hilda for a day or so. We managed to get our limit of birds in the very first day.

The following year, Shirley and I were back with the boys, hunting pheasants near Brooks. It had been a wet fall and a lot of the grain was left on the ground because it had been too wet to harvest it. One of the farmers was flooding his fields with irrigation water and the ducks were coming in like crazy.

We got permission from the farmer to hunt there, and before dark the four of us positioned ourselves in different places around the field. We were hiding the best we could, hoping to get some good shots. Kevin, who was ten that year, was about two or three hundred yards from us with the single-shot 20 gauge, and I saw two ducks circling around him. Just as they were about to land, Pow, down they both came.

"How come you let those ducks circle for so long before you shot them?" I asked him later.

"I was trying to get them lined up because I only had one shot and I thought I could get them both with the one shot." Well, that's exactly what he did.

The next day, we were at the top of the same field, along an irrigation ditch that had a lot of brush on either side. When we were hunting ducks the day before, we could hear pheasants along the ditch, so the next day we decided to hunt them. We got permission from the farmer, who said it was okay to hunt all along the ditch south of his property. "Don't go across the ditch and hunt in the alfalfa field or the fellow who owns it will be most upset."

The four of us went up the field and scared some pheasants

up. When we ran after them, Kevin disappeared. There was a place to get across the irrigation ditch, so Kevin crossed over to the other side. Shirley, Brian and I ran down the ditch chasing the birds, which flew off into the alfalfa field. Then we heard shooting way off in the distance.

Kevin had gone in the alfalfa field with a little Cocker spaniel he had that was great at rooting out birds. I heard quite a few shots and went into the alfalfa field to find Kevin and reprimand him. But he had five pheasants, so it was hard to give him too much of a chewing out.

"Hey, Dad," he said. "There are some more of them in there."

"Oh, are there now?" I said. I looked around and didn't see any farmers to give us shit. "Go get them," I told him. We both ran into the alfalfa and got three more. I let him shoot one of them and I shot the other two. We caught up to Shirley and Brian a couple of hours later, and they had four.

Today when you shoot pheasants in Alberta, nine out of ten are hatchery birds that have been released for hunters. The Brooks area has gone all to hell, and I don't know why there are not many wild pheasants there.

They had a go at shooting hens for a few years in some areas. The first time we tried for hens, we got nothing. After we figured out how the procedure to control hen hunting worked, we went hunting outside the area a couple of days later and got four or five hens. We hid them in my truck and we drove to the area where hen hunting was allowed. They stopped us and we got a permit to go into the area and hunt hens. We managed to get one more, and on the way out we showed the game warden the ones we had shot elsewhere, along with the one we just got. The guy said, "You did quite well. That's the best anyone has done today."

They call Brooks the pheasant capital of the world. If it wasn't for the fact that they have a pheasant hatchery there wouldn't be any pheasants around there. They raise three or four hundred thousand pheasants a year and turn them loose.

We found the areas where they released the pheasants. You are not allowed to hunt in these areas after two o'clock on the days they release birds, to give them a chance to scatter and adjust to being loose. One day we lingered until a lady came down the road with a truck full of crates of pheasants.

I buttered her up, trying to find out what the score was. She was having a hard time opening the lock on the gate into the field where she was going to release the birds. I got the lock open for her, and sprayed some oil into it.

"You can't come in to see me release the pheasants," she said. "But when I go down the road to the other place on the corner, you can watch me do it there." We went and waited for her, and eventually she came along in her truck.

She opened up the crates and let the pheasants out. There were about fifty of them, and when she set them loose they flew toward our truck, landing on the front of it, on the road and all around us.

"I do this every day at three o'clock," she said. "Don't forget, you are not allowed to hunt here until tomorrow morning."

"Oh, don't worry about that," I told her. Down the road she went. Well, when she was out of sight, a couple found their way into the back of the truck—dead. Another case of Ha, Ha, Ha. Down the road we went.

The next morning five of us went back there and loaded up with pheasants. Knowing where they are has a great deal to do with how many pheasants you get in Alberta. You could run up and down those fields all day long, and be lucky to see a hen, let alone a cock.

In the mid-'60s I bought myself a boat, a seventeen-foot Uniflite with a forty horsepower Westbend outboard engine. I used it to do a bit of fishing around Nanaimo. Not long after I got it, BC Ferries ran the *Kiloche* up on Snake Island. They were lucky. They hit the north end of the island which goes up at an easy slope. If they'd hit the Nanaimo end of it, it would have been a disaster. I jumped in my Uniflite and roared out for a look. It sure looked funny with more than half the length of the boat up on the island.

One time, just after I bought the boat, Brian and I were going to go fishing. A fellow had borrowed the boat just before this and told me he'd filled up my gas tanks. I backed down the boat ramp to put the boat in the water. I checked the tanks, but didn't notice that Brian took the rope off the back end of the boat. Like all my boys, he was an eager beaver who liked to get on with whatever we were doing.

I saw we didn't have any gas so I told him to jump in the truck and we'd go and get some gas. We went back up the ramp and over to what used to be the BA service station, which is now a Petrocan station. We filled the tanks and were coming back. I guess I was in a bit of a rush to get out fishing, and when I turned onto Stewart Avenue, the boat fell off the trailer. By the time I got stopped I'd dragged it down the road fifty yards or more. It put a hole in the side of this brand new boat.

I wasn't at all happy about that. "Hey, you took the rope off," I said to Brian. "Yeah, I thought we were going fishing."

"We were," I said. "But look at it now." I was wondering what we were going to do, when a bunch of pals of mine came along and between us all we lifted the boat back on the trailer. I had no boat for over a week while it was repaired. That wasn't the only instance with Brian taking a rope off.

There was a fellow looking to get a job from me, a Hungarian who had immigrated here. At that time I didn't have any jobs. While I was talking to him, I'd mentioned I'd like to have a little eight-foot dinghy or something to carry on top of my truck, made out of plywood. So he said if I bought the materials he'd make it for me. Great. I bought him the materials and he made me this nice eight-foot boat. He brought it down to the mill and put it on the roof of my truck, upside down, and tied it on with a rope.

I went home for lunch out to Long Lake. I lingered for a while and when I saw how late it was, headed back to the mill. I didn't notice that Brian had climbed up on the roof and taken the rope off the boat. Down the road I went and I was in a big rush because I was the sawyer and I hated to be paying those other guys when no wood was being cut. Just on the Nanaimo side of the golf course there was a fellow coming toward me and I saw him swerving to the left and point at the boat. I looked in the rear view mirror just in time to see the boat crash down on the road behind me. A couple of cars managed to swerve around it. I had been going about seventy-five or eighty miles an hour. The wind got underneath it and sailed it off the roof rack. It was smashed to pieces and there wasn't a thing worth saving. I kicked it in the ditch, got back in the truck and went off to work.

A day or so later the Hungarian fellow came along and asked if I got the boat painted. I said No, it was smashed to rat shit and I left it up along the road. Oh, he says, get me some more wood and I'll make you another boat. So he did. We gave him some work for a while, but it didn't work out.

On Friday nights in Nanaimo, if we weren't hunting or fishing, us fellows quite often went to Chinatown to eat at the Wongs. On one of these occasions there was a young fellow there, about nineteen years old, who was making a bunch of trouble and being a smartass. He was a tall, skinny kid, a spoilt hippy-looking brat with long black hair down past his shoulders. This night he mouthed off to me so I gave him a couple of whacks, chucked him on the floor, and sat on him. Johnnie was with me and I said "Johnnie, give me your knife."

He wanted to know what for. "I'm giving this hippie looking bastard a haircut." "No way," Johnnie said. "I'm not giving you the knife."

"Johnnie, if you don't give me that knife I'm going to get up off this floor and hammer you." So Johnnie gave me his knife. He was like me, we always had sharp knives.

"You keep still or I'll cut your bloody throat," I told the kid. I cut off big handfuls of his greasy hair. After I got up a friend of his came over and started giving me a bunch of shit for being so rough on this guy. I told him to mind his own business.

I noticed the kid had something in his hand that I thought was a knife. I made a grab for it and it went clean through my palm, between my thumb and the palm of my hand. It was a spring nail file. I gave a great reef and broke it right off. It was still sticking out of the back of my hand.

I didn't even bother to pull it out. I dumped that guy on the ground and hammered the stuffing out of him so he wasn't about to pull anything else. If he'd have stuck that nail file in my guts I probably wouldn't be here today.

When we hunted geese in Alberta, digging pits was a big job that sometimes took hours. At first we dug them by hand, and later on we blasted them out, but it was always a lot of work. One Sunday morning Ken Olsen—who owned the land we hunted on and liked to hunt with us—and I were driving down the road in his pickup truck. There was a two-foot auger, about five feet long, lying at the side of the road. It belonged to either the telephone or hydro people.

"Let's get that auger," I said to him. "We can rig that up on the back of your tractor and dig pits with it. Let's take it."

"We'll get in shit for that," he said.

"Let's take it under the lend lease plan," I told him.

"What the hell's the lend lease plan?"

"We'll just take it and then forget to take it back." He howled like crazy. We jumped out and it was heavy but we hucked it into his pickup truck and headed back to the barn. In a couple of hours we rigged the auger up to the power takeoff on his tractor.

It worked like a damn. We dug a lot of goose pits with that thing. We always dug them at night so we didn't have to worry about anybody seeing us. We used to watch the geese until about seven, then they'd fly away. We'd come back in the dark and dig our holes, then go back to hide the auger. It was the greatest thing we ever had. A two-foot hole would fit most of us fellows. We drilled down and a couple of guys shoveled away the dirt as fast as they could. Instead of taking two or three hours to dig each hole, if we had six or eight holes we'd auger them out in an hour and away we'd go.

One time, a couple of years after we got the auger, we loaded the tractor in Ken's truck and drove to the White farm. The digging was very tough there. It was a rocky place and we sheared off four or five shear pins before we got the holes dug. Then we loaded the tractor into the truck and hauled it back to the Olsen farm. Ken drove the truck, with the tractor in it, through the barn doors. They weren't high enough and we ripped out most of the gable end of the barn with the tractor. It screwed things up something awful. Before that hunting trip was over we spent quite a few hours fixing up the barn.

Although we didn't have a great hunt that day we did get thirty-three geese. When we were sitting in the pits waiting for the geese to come in a herd of forty-nine antelope came up to our decoys. It was a nice sunny morning. When we heard the geese coming we scared the antelope away because we didn't want them to scare the geese.

Two of the Bajich boys were with us on that hunt. When the geese came in and we started shooting we wounded some. We couldn't see them so my son Brian and Frank Bajich went after the wounded geese. I heard a few shots and then a weird sound.

"Uh oh," I said. "There goes somebody's gun barrel!" The others wanted to know how come I knew that.

"I'll never forget that sound. Brother Fred did it about thirty years ago when we were kids, up at Errington. That's the sound of a blocked up barrel exploding." Sure as hell, there came Frank Bajich with his gun looking like a musket. He'd been running across the field after the geese and poked the barrel in the mud. He didn't notice, and when he fired a shot, the barrel blew up. Luckily, no one got hurt. I had an extra gun, so he was able to use it and keep on hunting.

My friendship with the Olsons went on for eight years. We stayed on their farm and hunted there. He came out to visit me and I took him out fishing several times.

I was there once with my friend Harlan and Don McGillvery, along with Shirley, Brian and Kevin. We'd been hunting geese in the same field for three days and had great success. We were thinking about going home the following day and we were all doing a lot of drinking, especially Don.

Late that afternoon I was hunting the fence line, as there were too many in the pits as it was, especially given the amount of drinking going on. I shot a duck and it lit in the neighbor's grain field. When I walked in to get it the farmer came at me with a shovel and told me to get out of there. I told him I just wanted to get my duck, and a goose that had gone in there too.

He wouldn't let me get them, so I called him an old potlicker and walked away.

I got back to my truck and Shirley started giving Don and I shit for being so drunk. We climbed up a ladder onto the top of my truck and got into a boat that was on the roof rack. Shirley was driving, following Olsen across the field, and was going pretty fast. She hit a bump and Don flew out of the boat, fell on the ground and hurt his back.

I got Shirley stopped and we got Don into the truck, and back to the farm. Don was swearing and cursing at Shirley for driving so fast, and he and Harlan had words over that. Don punched him and gave him a bloody nose. At one point Don fell over backwards, into all the guns that were stacked in a corner. I grabbed his arm to pull him up and I guess it hurt his back some more. He charged me and down the stairs we went into the basement. Olson and a neighbour of his pulled us apart.

The Olsons were pretty upset. Shirley said "We're leaving here right now." We gathered up all our stuff and drove to Medicine Hat, where we found a motel.

The following year I phoned Ken Olson to see whether we were welcome or not. We weren't welcome, so we didn't stay there any more. After that we went to a farm about thirty miles away, the White farm, where we stay to this day. That was the end of the Olson friendship. I see Ken now and again, hunting pheasants and we're still on talking terms, which is better than not talking.

One summer I was coaching a kids' ball team in Nanaimo. On one of the game nights about six or seven kids were at my place waiting for a ride to the game. I'd spent a little too much time drinking beer and got home late. I didn't have time to eat supper, but jumped in the car with Shirley and the kids, with her driving. Down the road she went, roaring through a radar trap at fifty miles an hour in a thirty mile an hour zone.

Just at that point one of my kids said, "Oh, I forgot my glove." Shirley rammed the car in reverse and headed down the road backwards at about forty miles an hour, back through the radar trap. The cop stopped us and came over to the car. "You know, woman," and he was laughing. "You're the first person

I ever saw to go through radar breaking the speed limit going forward, and then go through it again over the limit in reverse. What's your problem?"

She told him about the kid forgetting his glove, and that we were late for the game. "You go home and get the glove," he said. "And drive properly. It won't make any difference now if you're late. I find this pretty funny, so I'll let you go. Away you go."

At the same time I was coaching this ball team, I was involved in a trap shooting competition at the Nanaimo Fish and Game Club. The ball team was playing in the BC championships, which were held in Nanaimo that year. I'd got myself involved in both things and had to spread myself pretty thin running back and forth between the ball game and the trap shooting competition.

We were winning the ball game and I was coaching third base. With all the running between events, I had got myself mixed up. It was the last inning with a tied score, and I thought we had two away, when in fact there was only one out. When the batter hit the ball I told the runner on third to boot it for home, and he got put out. The next batter hit a grounder into right field, and if we'd still had that runner on third he would have easily made it home and we would have won the game. Me telling him to run made us lose the championship.

In the 1960s I would sometimes buy some standing timber for the mill and get the Morgan brothers to log it for me. Once I bought some trees at a spot on Hammond Bay Road, near Piper's Lagoon, at a sharp turn on the road. There were no houses there at the time, just a lot of trees. I said to Art Morgan, "You can't go log those trees unless you get at least $350,000 worth of liability insurance."

"Oh," he said. "What do I need that for?" I said a tree might fall across the road. "You've got a stack of wires there and somebody might be killed. You got to have liability to work in Nanaimo."

"Okay. I'll get it," he said. It took him about a week to get it, and the day he came into the office with it I told him to go ahead. He drove down to do the falling in his convertible. The very first tree he cut had some rot in it. He lost control of the tree and it went down on top of his convertible, right across the driver's seat. The tree was about three feet through where it hit the car. It drove the frame of that car right into the ground. All the wires were down, and the road was blocked. What a hell of a mess.

One place I had a lot of luck hunting deer in those days was on Green Hooker Mountain, up in Nanaimo Lakes. I was up there in 1968 with Brian and Kevin. It had been storming this morning; it was early in the hunting season. We went up by the Teepee Bridge and away up onto Green Hooker. Up near the top I stopped for a minute. Away behind us I spotted a deer with the sun shining on it, just like a picture. I squared the truck around and took aim right out the window. It was about 400 yards away.

"What do you think," I said to Brian. "Should I shoot about a foot high?" He said yes. The deer was standing with its head to the left, broadside to us. I went whack and down came the deer. Kevin and Brian went over and dragged the deer down. It took about an hour to get it to the road. The boys were just as excited as I was, maybe more so. It was a lovely five pointer. That was one of my flukey deer kills.

With my boys and my pals I did a lot of hunting on that mountain. I first heard about it from an old sawyer friend of mine, Clarence Morten. He told me how to get there. Nearly every time we went up there we got a deer. It was one of our favourite places.

It was at Nanaimo Lakes, on Crown Zellerbach's land, and you couldn't drive in to the mountain because they had a locked gate on the road. The adjoining property was owned by M&B, but there were no roads between the two camps.

We would drive through the slash from the Crown side, over to the M&B land, in my four-wheel-drive truck, which was one of the first ones around Nanaimo. We weren't supposed to be there, but we never ran into anybody except someone else who shouldn't have been in there.

Before I got the truck, we used to walk in to hunt on Green Mountain. I was hunting there one time with Frank Denton and his young boys, George and Tom. Frank took his bicycle through the slash and went down one of the logging roads. He shot himself a four-point that weighed 174 pounds. I think that was the biggest deer we ever shot on Green Mountain. Frank tied it onto his bike and pushed it up the road. Then he came through the slash with it. The rest of us saw him and went to give him a hand. That's the only bicycle deer we ever got.

My kids used to call Frank "Frank the Rank" because he would get mad at them and holler and scream at them. George and Tom, and their brother David, even though they came from a cranky father, turned out to be great fellows. I don't mean to put Frank down; he worked for me for quite a few years and I miss him. Along with a lot of other pals older than me, they're all dead. Except for the two flatlanders, Willie and Fred. All that hard work on the farm must be what kept them alive so long. I don't think any of my friends made it to seventy-five. They all died quite early in life, in their late 60s and early 70s.

When Brian turned eighteen we went up to Green Hooker. It was late in the season, and snowing. We were on one of the hills, going along in the timber. He went down below me, and every once in a while he'd give a little whistle and I'd whistle back so we knew where each other were. A deer came running through the trees. It saw me and ran toward Brian. I gave a whistle and he whistled back, so I knew the deer was going to go behind him.

Some time before this I had been talking to Jackie Patterson, telling him about all the times I shot at deer running through the timber, but only hitting trees. He said what he always did was to watch where the deer was running. He'd pick out an opening ahead of the deer and put the gun on that.

I knew I could shoot without getting Brian with a ricochet so I did just what Jackie told me. Down went that deer, a bloody five pointer. Brian heard it coming down the hill and went back to where it was. He turned to me and said "I'm eighteen now. You shoot them and I'll pack them. You've been packing all my deer 'til now." He picked it up and packed it all the way to the truck, while I took the guns. Previous to that I used to carry the deer and he'd carry the guns.

One year in late November Alex Gerring asked Ken Olsen, Curley Chittenden and I to go hunting with him at Edson, Alberta. He was in the oil business there and had all sorts of equipment for getting around in the bush.

Curley and I were supposed to meet Olsen in Calgary, the morning after we finished some business at a loggers' meeting in Vancouver. That night after the meeting Curley and I got kind of mixed up, drinking and so on, and had a room at the Ritz Hotel.

We ended up with a couple of girls coming up to visit us in our room about 1:30 in the morning. We had encouraged them, of course. After a couple of drinks I took the prettiest one into the bathroom and after a few preliminaries I got around to sticking my hand in her pants.

Well, lo and behold. She had a cock and a pair of balls. "Curley," I yelled. "Check yours, this one's a boy." The other one was a girl but, anyway, we threw their shoes and panty hose out the window and sent them packing down the stairs.

We lay on the bed having a couple more drinks, still in our suits and ties, laughing about one of them being a boy. We went to sleep and when I woke up it was ten after seven. We're still in the same position and kind of pickled. I gave Curley a kick in the head and he jumped up, shaking his curly head and laughing. "Hey, didn't we have fun last night," he said.

"It was good for a laugh, mate. You want another bloody laugh? The goddamn plane left for Calgary at seven o'clock and its now a quarter after seven. We missed the bloody plane and that's the only one there is today."

"Holy Christ," he said.

I started phoning around and the only plane I could get was one into Edmonton. I knew when Olsen's plane was coming into Calgary so I called the airport and paged him. He said he'd meet us at the airport in Edmonton. By the time we got on the plane we'd had a few drinks and were pretty giggled up. We were acting up a bit and when one of the stewardesses asked us what we were going to do with the guns we had in our baggage, we told them we were going to shoot flying moose out the window. They didn't like that too much, so they told the Captain. He came back and gave us shit. He told us not to talk like that on the plane because it was upsetting other people, which it was. We cooled down a bit and he said to us we would have trouble flying home on the same airlines. Anyway, we got into Edmonton that night, and drove up to Edson to meet Alex.

By the next afternoon we got ourselves organized. This guy had all the equipment you could think of—Bombardiers, trucks, tracked machines—you could cross ice only an inch and a quarter thick. Alex often had guys there from Imperial Oil in there hunting, and there were a couple of them this day.

We went out scouting around that afternoon and came across a herd of fifteen elk. We let the Imperial Oil guys and Olsen take the shots and they fired fifteen times and didn't get anything. The next morning Alex got me up at four o'clock. The previous afternoon it had been fifteen degrees above; now it was thirty below. All the vehicles were frozen up and you couldn't move anything. It took until about eleven in the morning to get them thawed out.

While that was happening, Alex said "Come on. You and I'll go spot some animals in my plane. It's got an electric plug in it. It'll start." We got in the plane and warmed it up for the longest time before we took off. You couldn't believe the animals we spotted from that airplane. I never knew there were that many moose in the country.

When we came back the others had all the equipment running and we went out. Again we let the others do the shooting. Alex and I went into the bush and chased the animals out and let the others do the shooting. One of the guys from Imperial Oil managed to wound this huge moose and we chased it for two days before we finally got it. It had sixty-six inch horns. After chasing it for two days and being that old you can imagine what that meat tasted like.

After that Alex said he and I had better start doing some shooting. The next morning he, Ken Olsen and I were driving along in a power wagon and came on five moose in a clearing in front of us. We jumped out, gave those moose a barrage, and down they all went. The last one was a calf. I yelled at the others to stop shooting at it, because I could see it had been hit two or three times. It was just standing there like a sawhorse. I'd seen a deer do that a year or so before near Elko. It was dead standing up. We started walking toward it and it fell over, dead.

At one point Alex sent me off the road into the bush about 200 yards. He was going to chase some elk we'd spotted off the hillside toward me. I walked into the bush and found a spruce tree to hide behind, about eighteen inches through. I was waiting there with my .30-.06 when I heard Alex shooting. Then I heard the sound of something coming, and when I looked around the tree I saw a seven point elk booting it toward me. Instead of shooting when it was coming at me, because there were so many trees in the way, I waited, almost too long. When it got right opposite me, not thirty feet away it stopped behind a couple of little spruce trees.

I had my gun ready and thought "I can't shoot through that bush." While I was thinking about what to do, the elk leaned forward and looked around at me. I shot it right in the ear, pow. Over it went.

Then I heard Alex fire again and, running in the same tracks as the seven point, was a young spike. It went past the one laying on the ground, then put the brakes on, turned around and started licking its face. I shot it in the ear and it went down, their two noses together.

"I know you got them," he said. He could see the big smirk on my face. He'd got the cow.

The next morning he and I went out spotting again in the plane and found a big herd of elk we decided to go after. We loaded up the Bombardiers on a flat deck truck and headed into the area. There were seven of us that day and we all spread out from the road. I went off after the elk and was gone longer than anybody. When I came back, about two in the afternoon, I could hear these guys talking off to the right when I came back to the road, and I could smell they had a fire going.

Just as I hit the road I looked down it to the left, and there was a great big bull moose, with a cow, not even looking at me. They were right in line with a seismograph machine sitting down the road. I couldn't shoot because I was afraid I might hit the fellows working on the machine. I went off to the left, and the moose were crossing to the right. Once they got far enough over so I wasn't shooting down the road I shot and down went the bull.

I joined the others at the fire and had a sandwich and hot rum, while one of the guys walked down to where the dead moose was. We all got on the Bombardier to go and pick up my moose, and as we were going down the road, lo and behold, there was another bull moose. The guy who had walked ahead was in line with the moose, so we were afraid to shoot. We hollered at him and, fortunately, that was a dumb moose because it just stood there until he shot it. It doesn't happen too often that you get two moose in one day, let alone in one hour.

On the last day we decided we had time for one quick hunt, close to town. We went out and spotted a cow and calf moose lying down in a sawdust pile at an old sawmill. We went back and got the boys, one of them being Alex's father-in-law, an arrogant bloody German.

We told his father-in-law to go down the road a couple of hundred yards and to stay where we could see him. A couple of others went off to the left to circle the moose. The father-in-law went too far down the road and pretty soon we couldn't see him any more. Then we heard some shots and these moose came running toward where the father-in-law was supposed to be. But we couldn't shoot because we were worried about where the father-in-law was. If we could have seen him we could have shot.

After a while everybody came back, and the father-in-law was the first guy back to the truck. Alex said to me, "Hey George, you chew him out."

We were in the back of the truck when he came up and I said "If you would have stayed where we told you, you would have got those moose."

"Don't you tell me what to do you punker," he said. He was about ten years older than me. He pulled out his big hunting knife. "Otherwise I'll see how sharp my hunting knife is."

I took my .30-.06 and stuck it against his head. "Yeah? And I'll see how fast your head goes to bloody mush. Put that knife away." Alex chewed him out and that was the end of the hunting trip. In the end we got fourteen animals, and I shot nine of them.

Curley and I gathered up our meat, half a moose and half an elk each. Since we weren't allowed back on the plane, and because we had so much meat, we got on the train at Edson for the trip to Vancouver. We got first class tickets and right after we got on we walked into one of the bar cars. There were three guys sitting at the far end and we walked toward them with Curley in the lead. One of these guys made some smart-assed comment about "here comes a couple of wide-assed mounties" to Curley, who ran down the aisle and proceeded to punch the stuffing out of him. I kept the other two guys from getting up and when one of them got a bit wild I gave him one. That calmed him down. The conductor came and escorted us down to the first class bar, and that was the end of that. The rest of the trip was quite enjoyable.

In 1967 Bob Malpass, Ted Osbourne, Jack Wilson and myself went to the island of Dominica in the Leeward Islands. We had a chance to get a couple of billion feet of timber—gommier, which is much like mahogany. I went down there and was quite impressed with the timber. When I got back I talked to somebody in Vancouver who had been down there and bought some of these logs up. They tried to put them through a gang saw in Vancouver and it didn't work very well.

"Hey," I said. "We've got to get some of these logs, take them somewhere and saw them. What I hear is that these logs are full of silica—volcano ash." The others suggested I get some of the logs. I agreed to go down there and see what I could do about getting them shipped and sawed somewhere.

I got some information off a Jewish fellow in New York who used to buy planking off me, two-and-a-half by tens. They used a lot of that in New York for floor joists in the bigger buildings. I phoned him and he told me he'd heard of some guys who cut up half a million feet of this stuff in Puerto Rico during the war to build landing barges. He gave me their addresses.

I went to Puerto Rico and talked with someone in their forest service, who told me where to find these guys. I flew to

New York and met them. One of them was a fighter pilot who flew off aircraft carriers during the war and the other one was a torpedo pilot. They got together after the war and started this business. They were hilarious to talk to, and it was great to hear about their escapades during the war. They were gung ho guys to have a drink with, snort her up and talk about war stories and girls. They told me to get some logs and bring them up to West Virginia. Get thirty-five or forty logs, they said. "We'll saw them up and kiln dry the lumber and see how this is going to work." Great. I came back to Nanaimo, and then went back down to Dominica where I managed to round up forty some-odd logs. I had a hell of a time to get them on a ship and out of there. I finally found a ship in Barbados, put the logs on the ship, and took them up to New York where these guys trucked them down to West Virginia.

They phoned me and said "We're ready to cut those logs whenever you get here." I took my camera and away I went. It was quite an eye opener for me, even though I'd cut a lot of logs, been a sawyer and built sawmills. These fellows had a little hardwood mill. They were able to cut down to one inch on the last cut on the carriage.

A fellow in Vancouver had given me some special, high-speed saw bits and I took them with me. The foreman at this mill said "Oh, we'll saw these logs up like nothing." He thought they'd be easy to cut.

"Oh no," I told him. "These logs are very abrasive. They've got a lot of silica in them." He didn't know what I was talking about.

"What do you want to cut them into, George?" the super-intendent asked.

"Just cut them all into one inch," I told him.

He sawed up the first log and that was okay, but he got half way through the second one and that was the end of that. That saw wouldn't cut anything. When we looked at the teeth they were all rounded off from the silica, just like they'd been sawing sandpaper.

So we put my teeth in the saw and he sawed up all those logs without even sharpening them. They stood up real well. That proved to me that these logs could be sawed. We shipped the lumber down to a place to kiln dry it. They figured it would take nineteen days to dry it because of the high moisture content. It had real twisted, interlocked grain and you couldn't dress it up. But it was real strong and was something to use in rough construction.

We picked up a little sawmill in Vancouver. It had been going to South America but that deal fell through so we bought it. The carriage was no good, so I went to Mainland Foundry and got it rebuilt. We still hadn't planed any of the wood but, after cutting up the first batch of logs, we decided to go ahead with it.

In September 1967, I went down there with a couple of carpenters I hired through an ad in a Vancouver paper, and another fellow from Nanaimo. We built an office and put in the foundations and footings for the sawmill. I had already sawed the lumber to build the mill at my mill in Nanaimo and sent it to Vancouver to have it Wolmanized because we had a termite problem in Dominica. The mill was all pre-fabricated in Nanaimo.

I came back to Nanaimo just before Christmas, and over the winter made sure the lumber for the mill was all together and the mill was rebuilt properly. We had to get motors from England because the voltage in Dominica was different than here. We bought them from a retired Colonel in Dominica, who also sold us a D6 Cat that had been built in England. His stepson took us to Venezuela and showed us how they logged there. The forest service marked the trees and they selectively logged them using tractors that were constantly getting stuck. It was a real Mickey Mouse show, but it was an eye-opener to see how other people log.

We didn't have to do that. The government gave us a free hand and how we logged was our problem. Where we were logging it rained over 300 inches a year, so you can imagine what the mud was like. We had a shovel to build roads and a spar tree to log with. The loggers we had down there, we took from here. They were the worst bunch of drunken bums I'd ever seen.

Shirley decided she wanted to bring some of the kids to Dominica. Brian didn't want to go, but the other boys and

Darlene did. We all arrived there on April 17, 1968, and the following day two landing barges came in with all the equipment. It had come by rail to West Palm Beach, and then on these old World War II barges. They ran them right up on the beach. I had everything we needed to unload with right at the front.

We got to work on the mill and by June 2 it was running. Shirley, the kids and I moved into an old plantation house. It was a great old house with big four-poster beds. It was a nice experience to live there. It was a three-quarter hour drive to the mill. We worked twelve hours a day, so I drove there and back in the dark.

I had made a deal with my ex-aviator friends in New York. We were going to sell them the lumber at cost and they would sell it in the U.S. and develop the market for this species. After that they would start paying us a better price for it.

But Malpass and the others didn't want that. They wanted $170 a thousand for it, and it was costing us $140 a thousand to cut it. I argued with them about this. "That's not the deal we made. Those guys spent a lot of money on us. Let's play the game with them."

But, oh, no. Bob was going to sell the lumber. He'd never sold lumber in his life, and I'd been in it for twenty-odd years. The lumber wasn't getting sold. First, I built one big drying shed and we filled it up. It was all solid, clear wood. When we got that shed full, I built another huge shed. Pretty soon we had two sheds full of lumber. We had about two and a half million feet piled up, and we were running out of money.

I wanted to go ahead and start shipping it to these guys in New York but no, Bob's the boss. I started getting quite cranky and in late July 1968, I went home for the bathtub race and Shirley took the kids back.

In September I went back and couldn't believe the mess. When I left the sawmill was cutting 35,000 feet a shift. When I got back these guys had it down to about 20,000. I soon got them cranked back up again. We had trouble with the hired help down there. We didn't pay them all that much. They all thought they were mechanics. They could take power saws apart all right, then they'd lose half the parts. We were always getting more power saws, or getting parts to put them back together.

I had to get real heavy-handed with the loggers. A woman had a little wine and liquor store right up by where they were logging. These guys were drinking on the job every day and not getting their work done. They were even encouraging the natives to drink.

After I got things going again there was still no lumber being shipped. Bob was always out on what I called the Triangle Run. He'd go to Trinidad, New Orleans and Antigua. All he ever did was talk with a bunch of clowns who never did buy any wood from us. It was just a trip checking out the girls. He made this trip about once a week, so I hardly saw the man.

I got hold of the guys in Vancouver, Osbourne and Wilson, and told them they'd better get down there. "Look you guys," I told them, "if you want me to stay on running this sawmill, you better come down here. We need to get selling this lumber and honour our obligations to these fellows we were going to do it with in New York."

They came down, with a couple of women that weren't their wives, to have a meeting. They were down there holidaying for three weeks. They stayed in the most expensive place on the island and ran up huge bills that we couldn't afford. The bank was getting upset about our overdraft.

I set up a meeting for ten o'clock one morning in the office. We had a fridge full of fruit juices and vodka, so we had a couple of drinks. "Okay, let's get on with the meeting," I said. So, what's the story, they wanted to know.

"You see all that lumber out there?" I asked. "Then you see all the shit we're getting from the bank. You guys don't care because you're hiding in Vancouver." I had put up a personal guarantee of $60,000 to Mainland Foundry to get the sawmill fixed. I hadn't been paid yet, and had only taken $5,000 in salary out of the company to this point. I was quite vexed at these guys.

"The only way we're going to get any money happening around here is to sell this lumber. The sun's checking it, even though it's in the sheds."

"What do you want to do?" Osbourne asked.

"I want to be the supreme commander. I'm fed up waiting for Bob to sell lumber." So they turn to Bob and say "What do you think, Bob?"

"I'm the boss," he said. "You're not going to be supreme commander, Dorman." The others said, yeah, Bob's the boss.

"Okay," I said. "The meeting's over. Let's have a drink."

We had a couple of drinks and at 11:30 one of them said "Hey, Dorman. Let's go and have some lunch and talk about this."

"Okay," I said. "But first I have to do something at the mill. I'll meet you there." They took off to this fancy hotel. I went to the mill and talked to my friend Andy Terrace, my head planer man. I told him what I was doing. "You're on your own. I'm going home. I've had enough of this."

I went over to the government office and cleared my immigration and customs status. They gave me a permit to leave the country. Then I went to the airlines office and got a ticket. I said goodbye to a couple of other guys, and went to the hotel.

I sat down and had a drink. They started in about me being so cranky. "Well, you guys are going to have fun, because I'm going to be on that plane at seven o'clock tomorrow morning."

"You'll have trouble clearing customs," Osbourne said right away. "And where are you going to get a ticket from?"

I pulled all of my papers and ticket out of my shirt pocket. "See, that, there they are. I don't have to listen to you guys any more."

Then they started suckholing. Malpass got me another drink. I drank it and said "Fellows, there's nothing further to talk about. I made my decision; you guys made yours. Sell that bloody lumber yourselves, and have fun." With that I took off. That night Bob came out to the plantation house and tried to talk me out of leaving. But that was it. I came back to Nanaimo the next day and started paying close attention to the chip mill.

I went back there at Mardi Gras time the following February and I couldn't believe it. Bob still hadn't sold much lumber. He did sell a shipload of logs to a Spaniard, which he never did get paid for. He lost three or four hundred thousand dollars there. When I went over to the sawmill they were down to 18,000 feet a day, in two shifts. When I was there, we had sixty-five loggers in the bush. Now there were 130 and they couldn't keep up to the sawmill.

In the end the mill went broke and was bought by the French government. They moved it to French Guiana. Bob kept a fifty percent interest in it. After about a year he sold his interest to the French government and bought a gold mine. By this time Osbourne died. Bob died of a heart attack not too long later. And about a year later Jack Wilson died. I never got any of my money back. They had a hurricane in Dominica and it blew the office away. Now the land where it was located is an airport.

By 1971 my marriage to Shirley had turned into a disaster. It had lasted seventeen years. She had accepted my two daughters and we raised another five kids of our own. She was a hard-working lady, but in the early '60s she had a nervous breakdown and her mind was never the same again.

When I got up one morning and the kids had left for school, she sang to me :

"Hooray, hooray, the first of May.

It's going to be Shirley's moving day."

Then she said, "I don't love you any more George and I'm going to divorce you. I'll be your housekeeper until the kids are out of school in June, then you're on your own after that."

"Oh, great," I said. I noticed that my friend Don McGillvery had bunched his wife in February of the same year. Shirley moved out and we got a divorce. The following year, she and McGillvery got married and are still living together. They seem to have a war every day, but that's their business and I'll let them worry about it.

As for me, there I was at age forty-six, with five kids to raise and a sawmill employing 150 people that I was responsible for. How I survived that is another story.